To my friend of
many years —

Oremus pro invicem

Jerry Kenney

TRUST

JESUS

ISBN 1-885931-15-2

Library of Congress Cataloging-in-Publication Data

Kenney, Jeremiah F., 1939-
    Trust Jesus / by Jeremiah F. Kenney.
        p. 214   cm.
    ISBN 1-885938-15-2 (pbk.)
    1. Jesus Christ--Devotional literature. 2. Bible. N.T. Gospels--Devotional literature. 3. Spiritual life--Catholic Church.
    I. Title.
    BT306.5.K46   1998
    232--dc21   98-42322
                                                                               CIP

Published in 1998 by

Cathedral Foundation Press
P.O. Box 777
Baltimore, Maryland 21203

Publisher: Daniel L. Medinger
Assistant Manager: Patti Medinger
Book design: Lisa Wiseman
Cover design: Dave Schall
Front cover photograph: Dave Schall
Printed by: Catholic Printing Services

TRUST

JESUS

By
Monsignor Jeremiah F. Kenney

A short course in devotion:
That bridge between prayer and worship

Dedicated to my two Mothers,
the Marys of my life

Cathedral Foundation Press
Baltimore, Maryland

CONTENTS

....

....

FOREWORD

In these pages Monsignor Jeremiah F. Kenney, a priest of the Archdiocese of Baltimore, couples rhetorical skills developed as a teacher of the English language with pastoral approaches enriched in parish, tribunal and chaplaincy settings. His reflections are the fruit of more than a quarter century of faithful and deeply committed priestly service.

May the reader be inspired by Monsignor Kenney's enthusiasm for the basics of the spiritual life and his sense of the love which the intercessory prayer of Jesus has for us and of the power of Mary, the holy Mother of God.

Cardinal William H. Keeler
Archbishop of Baltimore

INTRODUCTION

"The Acts of Jesus," published in 1998, reputed to be the work of "biblical scholars" from Santa Rosa, California, gave as their "verdict" that Jesus Christ "... did very few of the actions ascribed to him." In fact, of the 176 events catalogued, the members of the "Jesus Seminar" concluded that only 28 actually occurred with any "historical probability." So said a report in a major daily newspaper!

When I read the lengthy article, I had to ask myself why a group of supposed scholars would bother to research a life that they concluded was almost totally fiction! I thought to myself how utterly foolish to spend such enormous quantities of time, talent and treasure doing "research" into the life of a "thirtyish year old" carpenter from the backwater village of Nazareth who lived 2,000 years ago and who, by their own admission, " ... (Jesus) lived, as a person executed during the prefecture of Pontius Pilate (A.D. 26 to A.D. 36), ... after some incident at the Temple ... (that) he was crucified at a place called Golgotha, ... he was flogged in accordance with Roman practice (and) his disciples fled when he was arrested ..." That's it!?!

So some 75 "biblical scholars or fellows" found that "the notion that the disciples of Jesus found an empty tomb on Easter morning to be unlikely." They called the whole Jesus Christ event "pure Christian propaganda" which happened to develop in Galilee where (at the time) the two new religious movements, Rabbinic Judaism and Christianity, were just emerging and intense rivalry produced hostility that left its mark on these stories.

After reading the well written article in the newspaper,

I began to make my usual daily holy hour. For most of my religious and priestly life, first as a religious brother of the Congregation of Holy Cross and then as a Baltimore archdiocesan priest, I had always spent an hour or more alone with the Eucharistic Lord Jesus. I was deeply troubled at the damage the article would do to the faith of some people going through the traumas of life with little but their faith upon which to hang their lives! I had just returned from Alabama where I had been on EWTN's "Mother Angelica Live" and had been the principal celebrant and homilist at the conventional televised Mass the following morning.

Deeply touched by the questions of the viewers and by the many letters from people all over the world, I decided to write this little book about the motto which has formed the basic structure of my life: Trust Jesus!

In the book, I have tried to take gospel cameos and reflect upon them. These cameos are from the New Testament, from the life of Jesus Christ. I have tried to explain what must have happened during the event; I have attempted to bring the events to life. Then, in the second section to each of the chapters, I attempt to engage the Lord Jesus in dialogue. The Lord speaks first and tells the reader (or listener) about His own feelings and attitudes with reference to the cameo event. The reader then has the opportunity to speak to and with Jesus. This makes for an event we call contemplation. In the event, the reader has a wonderful opportunity to grow in understanding of life with Jesus. Keep in mind that love is based on knowledge of the Beloved of Jesus Christ. Having heard and experienced Jesus we now may "interact" with Him and grow more deeply in our own dependence on Him and His values.

You see, through acts of adoration, reparation, thanksgiving, and petition we make our wills and desires known to

God. Through these actions we bring forth our whole lives, our emotions, and invest them in a relationship with Jesus. Next, we learn to listen to Him; we learn to hear His pain, His sorrow, His joy and happiness. This makes it possible for us to dispose ourselves to doing God's will. God's will isn't easy! It's hard! To accomplish doing God's will we need to invest ourselves in devotion, i.e., emotionally, spiritually, intellectually and even physically, we need to "watch and pray" with Jesus. Out of this "watching and praying" is born our practical resolutions. These resolutions will help us to better live our faith in Jesus, the object of our trust!

For this reason alone, and from the encouragement of many friends and family, I have set pen to paper (I'm not too good with a computer!) in order to give some reflection into the life of the object of my love, my closest friends, the Lord Jesus Christ and His Blessed Mother, my mother and yours. I hope you will profit from this work.

CHAPTER ONE

Who is Jesus?
From where did He come?

The Gospels of Matthew (1:1-17) and Luke (3:23-24) give us a look at the genealogy of Jesus Christ. Beginning with Abraham we see the long lineage of Jesus Christ through the paternal line. The names of Isaac, Jacob, Judah, Perez, Hezron, Ram, Aminadab, Nakshon, Solomon, Boaz (by Rahab, a prostitute!), Obed (by Ruth), Jesse, King David, Solomon (by the wife of Uriah), Rehoboam, Alijah, Asa, Jehoshaphat, Joram, Uzpiah, Jotham, Akaz, Hezchiah, Manasseh, Amos, Josiah, Jechoniah (the time of the Babylon deportation); Shealtiel, Zerubbabel, Abiud, Eliakim, Azor, Zadok, Achim, Eluid, Eleazar, Matthew, Jacob who was the father of Joseph, the husband of the Blessed Virgin Mary of whom Jesus Christ was born.

During her great pregnancy, when nine months pregnant, she traveled from Nazareth to Bethlehem, Judea, in order to register so as to fulfill the command of the Emperor. The various Old Testament references are Isaiah 7:14, 8:8; Numbers 24:17; Micah 5:2; Isaiah 60:6; Hosea 11:1. Together with her husband Joseph, Mary went to Bethlehem because she was a good person, faithful to the wishes of the authorities. She was always caring, insightful and totally other-conscious.

When the great Messenger of God, Gabriel, asked her to become the mother of the Messiah, she was startled! She proved her great intelligence by asking a profoundly insightful question for a young girl around the age of 15 years. "How can this be since I do not know man?" (Luke 1:26-38). To "know man" meant to have an intimate knowledge of man. Mary realized fully that she needed God's help. She never became overwhelmed at the presence of the Archangel. She responded in a calm, understanding and respectful way, quite a great undertaking for an adolescent in any day and age!

When I think of this period in the life of Jesus Christ, my mind ponders the Blessed Virgin – Mother. She's told she is to be the mother of Emmanuel (God is with us) (cf. Luke 1:23); almost immediately after the birth of Emmanuel she must flee to Egypt because her child's death was ordered by a mad king (cf. Luke 2:13-18). Even in the holiest of places, the Temple in Jerusalem, holy Simeon tells her she " ... shall be pierced with a great sword – so that the thoughts of many hearts may be laid bare." (cf. Luke 2:35).

Why? Why all this pain? For one reason: so that the good could win over evil; so that God's will and His way could prevail! What a terrible price for anyone to pay; and Mary could not have been more than seventeen years old when she heard these awful words of Simeon!

I don't doubt that the heavens were joyful and that a great multitude of angels were present to the shepherds. I would never doubt that as Luke says they praised God in song saying: "Glory to God in high heaven, peace on earth to those on whom His favor rests." (cf. Luke 2:14). What I really wonder about is Mary and the profound effect this had on her!

We see her shortly after the Annunciation and Incarnation, in the earliest part of her pregnancy visiting Elizabeth – her parent's cousin, a woman great in age and advanced in pregnancy. Recognition, redemption and peace are reflected in this beautiful cameo from the earliest moments of her pregnancy. Her canticle, her magnificat tells us all we need to know about her and her Son! (cf. Luke 1:46-55). Truly, she is profoundly happy! She has no "mistaken notion" about who she really is! Fully aware, fully appreciative, she "explodes" into the most beautiful prayer any creature could pray:

"My being proclaims the greatness of the Lord,
my spirit finds joy in God my savior,
For He has looked upon his servant in her lowliness;
all ages to come shall call me blessed.
God who is mighty has done great things to me,
holy is His name; ... "

Mary is singing her faith in God the merciful!

She calls for a deep appreciation of God's mercy. This appreciation and respect is called "fear of the Lord." It takes place every time I try to avoid sin because I love and respect God's will for me. It takes place when I take chances and risks in order to witness to my faith. When I refuse to tell a "dirty joke" or use the Holy Name in a careless and disrespectful way; when I say something positive about my neighbor when so many others are saying uncharitable and unkind things about the neighbor – this is true "fear of the Lord" lived and practiced!

Mary realized that we are all sources of responsibility and as such will one day need to render an accounting of our thoughts, our words and our deeds. She gave all credit for true justice to God:

"He has shown might with His arm;
He has confused the proud in their inmost thoughts.
He has deposed the mighty from their thrones
and raised the lowly to high places.
The hungry He has given every good thing,
while the rich He has sent empty away ... ."

I truly believe, the whole moral teaching of Mary's Son is found in these verses! These words, Mary's own, from her "pondering heart," speak to us of Jesus and the lessons He taught as He walked the hills, valleys and villages of His country. One thinks of His teaching on humility and mercy, teachings found in Luke's gospel, chapters 14 and 15. These lessons are rooted in Mary's Son, her Magnificat! Jesus cured even on the Sabbath! He was the forgiving father in the story of the prodigal son. Yet, in both cases and in all other teachings and actions of Christ, Mary's Son demanded a change of heart from the learner, the cured, the disciples who hung upon His every word!

People who think themselves secure and comfortable will always have difficulty with Mary's words and Jesus' life. The manner and method of the Messiah and His Mother is always one of challenge! When we accept the challenge of the gospel, then, and only then, have we a right – under and with God's graces – to accept its comforts! The full impact of Mary's words can never be felt apart from Jesus' life and deeds! He is the totality of His mother as He is the totality of his Father! Just as the Holy Spirit came upon Mary, so the same Holy Spirit came upon Jesus, God's Eternal Word, to strengthen Him to set right the message so muddled by so many down through the ages! Just as that "clarifying, comforting Holy Spirit" brought about the birth of the Church in that upper room at Pentecost in a way that was sudden, complete and all-embracing, so in us today, that same God-given Spirit will clarify and help us to change into reflections of Jesus and Mary. The operating Spirit of the Father and Son is, I truly believe, uppermost in the prayer of the Mother always spoken and unspoken as she gazes into the glorified eyes of her Son.

Jesus is always Mary's Son; Mary's whole life! When I think of Mary, I look at Jesus; when I see Jesus, I look into Mary's eyes. The Son is never far from the Mother and the Mother is always near the Son! They are always present to each other, for each other and with one another. "To Jesus through Mary" is the way I believe God wants us to live. After all, didn't He send His Son to us through Mary? She was free; she could have said, no! Many women today shout no to the forming fetal life within themselves! What if she had said no to Gabriel? It cannot be, in my opinion, presumed that the redemption of the human race would automatically have taken place in another way! It cannot simply be assumed that still another woman would be asked to be the mother of the Lord! We have God the Father and the Blessed Virgin Mary to thank for Jesus. We have Mary, together with Joseph, to thank for the quality of life given Jesus as an infant, child, adolescent and man! The role of Mary and Joseph cannot be diminished by saying that God would have found still another way to accomplish our redemption had not Mary cooperated with the Divine will!

Who is Jesus? From where did He come? He is the Eternal Word; born in time; born of Mary; raised by Mary and her husband. To raise a person is the greatest challenge given a human being. To raise someone implies not only caring for them but loving them by being a constant example to them of what is truly the noble and good in the human condition. Mary is that norm against which all else in the life of Jesus – as man – is measured! Mary is that singular person in the life of those among us fortunate enough to have had or have a loving, all nurturing, all present-love we call mother!

Yes, only a mother truly understands her children from the inside out! Any mother reading these lines knows the totality of her gift to her own sons and daughters. Kids all demand the total presence of Mom. Youngsters' demands are never-ending and all-consuming. All mothers try. Some try harder than others. Few, in the vast scale of human history don't try at all. That is why today we are facing a new phenomenon with the "abortion mentality" already so deeply woven into the fabric of our culture. I often think that if anyone had the best reason for saying no to Gabriel it would have been an unmarried girl of 15-years-old! I wonder if today the young among us could take some time to think about this young unmarried girl and her Son. Think about what she accomplished and He accomplished! He died for us and redeemed us when we were lost and He did all of this from the moment He was conceived until He died at the age of 33 years! Imagine, a 15-year-old girl and a 33-year-old Man: two people who changed the destiny of the human race, and at such tender ages! Jesus Christ, Son of God, Child of Mary, one of the three Persons of the Most Blessed Trinity and, because of Mary, one of us! His genealogy, quoted earlier, had people of all sorts: saints and sinners, very ordinary and very extraordinary folks, people like you and me. How good God is to have made His Messiah come from real human roots, real human beings. The best of us can boast and the worst of us can brag that God belongs to each of us and all of us! He came from us to bring us to God so that we could share His life as the God-Man forever!

THE UNSPOKEN, THE HIDDEN

She must have been terrified when great Gabriel came. She must have thought: how should I act; what should I say; how should I respond? Who among us would not have felt this! Yet, she responded perhaps unlike us. She simply asked a question of clarification and threw herself into God's will! How did she tell her parents? What would any young girl do if she found herself pregnant outside of marriage? How many young girls today think to go to Mary in such stress? I can imagine what she would say and how closely she could identify with them. (Our Lady speaks.)

"Don't worry, I really do understand. Here ... let me hold you. Cry, get it all out ... I know how frightened you must be. I know how confusing it all is; I went through it myself and I was only 15! In my day there were horrible consequences, I could have been stoned to death! Like today, people thought the worst and often imposed the exact penalty required in our law. When I said I would have God's baby, I really didn't bother to consider all the consequences. I simply figured that God would show me the way and my true friends and family would help me get through. That's all! I just said to myself: I'll let God be God and do the best I can do. I'll love my baby and take good care of Him. I'll be sure that He will be brought up to practice our faith and I'll try to be near Him throughout our lives.

Of course, I never fully understood all that He meant when my husband and I went searching for Him. We found Him lost in the Temple! He was only 12! I'll never forget how He introduced us to God's plan for Himself and for us. He said: 'Do you not know I must be about My (heavenly) Father's business?' For many, many years I pondered what this meant. Only after His resurrection did I fully know that My Son is truly the way, the truth and the light of all the people, all over the world and at all times.

I want to tell you something: When they took those terrible large spikes out of His hands and feet and placed His rain-drenched bloody body in my arms I felt, through empathy, His every wound. I could only raise my eyes, drenched, soaked with tears to heaven and cry 'pity!' When we took His body to the tomb and I kissed Him for the last time – my heart was broken. John, Mary and some close friends helped me back to the house, to the upper room. In a corner of the room, John prepared a small cot and some privacy curtains for me. My eyes were closed, I couldn't cry any more. I couldn't speak; I hurt all over my body. I wasn't able to get comfortable despite every effort I could make. Finally, half in-and-half-out of sleep, unable to even lift the covers over me due to total exhaustion, I felt my eyes burning. John had forgotten to close the curtain and the bright light burned my eyes. But wait, I thought, the night couldn't have slipped by so fast! It can't be morning yet! I felt a warm hand holding my unwashed hand. I smelled sweet roses and spices, it was such a beautiful fragrance. Then I felt the closeness of His face. His soft beard caressed my skin. I awakened, rubbing my right eye with my free hand: "John? ... yes ... what is it? Is everything okay? Is it, John?" Then I opened my eyes. The room was clean and bright – but it was bright only in the corner John had prepared for me. I blinked ... and I blinked again ... Jesus! It was my boy! My Jesus! My heart pounded inside my chest. My eyes couldn't open wide enough to take Him all in. Jesus, I shouted ... You're alive!! He touched me, placing His finger over my mouth. I cried. I laughed. I wanted to scream, He's alive! He's here!!

Then He whispered to me: "Mother, Mom, I'm fine! Look at Me but be very quiet. The others need to sleep and I must yet do some more duties for the Father, your heavenly Spouse, before I will come to them. Mom, I just wanted you to know how I felt. I want you to know that I love you, Mom, and thank you for having been there for Me as you will always be there for all of My disciples. It was absolutely essential that I had to see you! My own joy of resurrection would be incomplete if I did not see you! You must never be sad again! I'm fine."

Then He kissed me, holding my head with His left hand and touching my cheek with His right hand. Suddenly, all my pain was gone. My body felt young again. I thought I could dance and jump for joy! My eyes were clear and I experienced a greater joy at that moment than I had ever experienced then or since. I knew from then on that things were going to be fine. I want you to know that My Son and I will never leave you. No door of life will ever be closed that tightly without us opening a window for you!

You see, we must always remember that we were not made for this life. We were made for heaven and heaven is right here and now, within you! Remember, a heart-beat from now, you will be before Jesus and the Father. Please pray as He taught you. Never lose hope or confidence in God. Look at what I went through! It all turned out fine in the end! Pray as often as you can. Pray and ponder the words you speak. Go slowly when you pray. Make acts of adoration, reparation for sins, thanksgiving and petition. Make them sincerely and quietly. Stop shaking and being resentful if your request isn't answered. Imagine Jesus always listening to you. When He listens He always gives what He thinks best for you. Try to incorporate His will in your life. Give your worst pain and loss to Him! He can make a grain of seed grow into a beautiful flower. He knows the place of every star and blade of grass. He knows you inside and out! Try to remember why you were made: to know Him here on earth so that you will be able to live in Him forever. Know that when you finally die your body will return to earth. Your soul and your spirit will be caught up, together with the souls of all the just, into the risen mystical Body of Jesus. That risen glorified Body is your heaven. It is totally united to the Word, the Eternal Son. In, with and through Jesus you will experience God. That is why the eye has not seen nor the ear heard nor has it ever entered the mind of man what God has prepared for those who love Him! Remember, at the resurrection on the last day, you will get a new body. That body will resemble Jesus' body and my body. Until then, Jesus will keep your soul and spirit and He and I will show you our home, now your home as well, a place we call heaven!

CONTEMPLATION – PRAYER

Jesus, living in Mary, come and live in me. Intensify your presence in me. Let me experience a renewed hope and confidence that you are my Brother and Redeemer. Let me know even now that Your kingdom is deep inside of me. Let me fully rest in Your sacred heart, filled with mercy for me. Jesus, I'm so scared at times. I feel so alone and lonely. I want and need someone to love me, to put his arms around me and hold me.

Lord, do not judge me but forgive me! I haven't invested myself enough in Your life! I haven't walked in Your shoes. I want You to walk in mine but I'm so selfish I haven't even tried to put Your shoes on me! Please, Lord, let me feel Your disappointment in me yet let me know of Your great need to love me! They say that in any relationship, the person who loves the lesser controls the direction and destination of the relationship. Lord, I know that Your love for me today, yesterday and always is far greater than my love for You can ever be.

Lord, help me to see into those areas of Your life hidden for so many years. Help me to quickly respond to the call of grace as You responded to Your Mother and Saint Joseph. Help me to be tough with myself in order to always do Your will as You did Your Father's will. I can't imagine what You went through knowing all You had to suffer as You left that last supper to go to Your agony and death. Your sweat became blood; Your body was beaten beyond recognition; Your head was crowned with thorns and Your closest friends would have nothing to do with You. I can't imagine how You felt nailed to the cross as You gazed upon Your dearest mother and Your youngest apostle. Helpless Yourself, You taught us how to help each other. Ever giving, You allowed

Your life to be spent so that we might live! Ever loving, Your love made-up for our selfish "me-first" love; Ever with us, You found a way to live within us: You gave us the Mass, the Holy Eucharist so that through the miracle of a transfiguration, a transubstantiation – (Divinity living in us) – we might glow and be for all the world that light which comes from heaven. That we might be You!

Jesus, I am Your family. You came from the human race; Your destiny is heaven where You want to live with Your family. Jesus, keep me always one with You! Jesus, let me know that nothing on earth will ever happen to me as long as I live in Your sacred heart.

Jesus, help me to fully appreciate the role of Your mother, Mary, in my salvation. You always loved her; You wanted John to love her and You want me to love her. Now, she cares for us as she once cared for You. Jesus, You alone know how much You needed her. You know as well how much I need her! Jesus, I love her and I want her to tell You how much I want to be in Your family. Give me Your Mother. Then I will truly be Your brother/sister.

For my part, O Blessed Mother, I give you every bit of myself. I give you my body, my mind and my spirit. Take me and raise me as you raised Jesus. Let me live in this world ready at a moment's notice to enter the next world. Remind me to pray to you. Whenever I see a beautiful sunrise or sunset; a blue sky or flowering field; feel a gentle breeze or a calm sea, help me to remember you, O Blessed Mother. Be inside me to guide me. Be outside of me to defend me. Be ahead of me to guard me. Be behind me to protect me. Be on my right side to direct me and be on my left side to give me safe rest. Dear Mother, watch over my thoughts. Keep them pure and filled with thoughts of your Jesus, your heaven and my destiny. When at last I go before God living in Jesus, let Him say to me that you have often spoken with love my own name to the Blessed Trinity: the Father, Son and Holy Spirit, our God, our destiny, our home now and always and forever and ever. Amen!

HIS WILL IN MY LIFE

I resolve that from this meditation, I shall try to be more conscious of the role of Mary and Jesus in my daily life. Especially in my waking moments, early in the morning, I shall remember to consecrate my daily tasks to the glory of God in honor of my relationship with Jesus, my Redeemer, Lord and brother and with Mary, His mother and my mother.

I shall remember that I live each day but a heart-beat away from that eternal encounter with God. Knowing that Jesus and Mary will speak on my behalf with the Father, I resolve never to do things which will shame me in God's presence and I shall do those good deeds and speak those positive words to others about others so that destructive criticism will no longer be a part of my life.

I promise that when I am wronged, I shall try to set aside all resentment and keep my mind from being disturbed. With God's help and Mary's prayers, I shall try not to allow one angry word to escape from my lips; I will strive always to be kind and friendly, with loving thoughts and no secret malice. Hope in God's ways rescues all of us in the end. I will be hopeful and avoid all resentment knowing that Jesus and Mary suffered far greater for me than I could ever suffer.

Finally, I pray that I will die as I try to live: with malice for none and good will toward all. Grant this prayer, Lord Jesus through Your Mother's love. Amen!

CHAPTER TWO

Jesus Christ and John the Baptist:
What was their relationship
and what does this
mean to me today?

We first hear of John the Baptist when the angel speaks to Zechariah the Old Testament priest while Zechariah was functioning as priest in the Temple. (cf. Luke 1:5-24). The Messenger of God gives clear instructions to Zechariah, who is called – together with his wife Elizabeth – "just in the eyes of God" (Luke 1:6). Elizabeth is to conceive, in the normal way, a son. The son is even given his name by the angel, John (Luke 1:1-3b).

Zechariah responds with doubt and disbelief: "How am I to know this? I am an old man; my wife too is advanced in age." (Luke 1:18). To say that the angel is a wee bit disturbed is to clearly understate the issue! He responded: "I am Gabriel who stands in attendance before God; I was sent to speak to you and bring you this good news. But now you will be mute – unable to speak – until the day these things take place, because you have not trusted my words. They will all come true in due season." (Luke 1:19, 20).

What a terrible consequence of refusal to incarnate God's holy will! What a totally different response than was had by Our Lady to God's messenger. Interestingly enough, both responded to the Divine will but how very differently! Still in the final analysis, God had His way with us and always will.

A most beautiful act of testimony is locked into the words of the now pregnant Elizabeth: "In these days the Lord is acting on my behalf; He has seen fit to remove my reproach among men." (Luke 1:25). Finally the two great women meet. Instantly, the unborn speak in quiet eloquence to one another. Next they – at least one of them, John, speaks through his mother as she says to the mother of the newly conceived Messiah: "Blest are you among women and blest is the fruit of your womb. But who am I that the mother of my Lord should come to me? The moment your greeting sounded in my ears, the baby leapt in my womb for joy. Blest is she who trusted that the Lord's words to her would be fulfilled." (Luke 1:42-45).

I cannot help but note that in the earliest state of her pregnancy, she is called "mother of the Lord"! Here, what could not have been any more than a thimble full of chemicals (at least from a physical point of view) is given all the rights of personhood! Addressing Mary directly, she calls Mary the "Mother of the Lord." She does not call her "Soon-to-be-the-mother-of-the-Lord"! Mary is immediately – some say within three days of the Gabriel event – called the Mother of the Lord – not the "mother" of chemicals! She is the mother of an unborn baby who, at this stage, reaches outside of His mother's womb to purify His cousin, John. John too is yet unborn!

Elizabeth continues: "The moment your greeting sounded in my ears, the baby leapt in my womb for joy." (Luke 1:44). How awesome! How terribly necessary for us today who are expected to live "in comfort" and conformity with the culture of death!

Two unborn children acting, communicating with each other! One the Word of God, the other, God's greatest voice! One the essence of the holy, the other the symbol of humanity being redeemed! One the Messiah, the other the greatest of the prophets! But both, unborn, obviously aware of their respective yet all-important roles! Both acting, communicating and doing those necessary things people do when the most important realities in life, of life, must be done!

John is born and Zechariah speaks in blessing of God! John is who he is, named by Gabriel as that mighty angel named his Cousin, Jesus. Named before conception as was his Cousin, John is to be that great voice crying in the wilderness of every day, place and time: "Make ready the way of the Lord, clear Him a straight path." (Luke 3:4b).

What beautiful words ... but what a greater sense of timing for us in our own age. The Word of God (Jesus) carried by the Voice of God John challenges each of us and all of us to pause and ask ourselves if the Lord's way in our lives is truly ready! Have we cleared Him a straight path? Are the valleys in our lives filled in and the mountains and hills leveled? Have the windings been straightened as the rough paths were being made smooth? For if they have not, we shall never see the salvation of God! (cf. Luke 3:4-6).

We see John, the Voice, the Man, the Prophet always working for God. John is all-present to the people of his day and age. His challenge is what is needed now. Often we seek out the comfort of the Gospel but never reflect, let alone live, the challenges of Gospel life! John confronts Herod, tetrarch (ruler) of the territory. He calls Herod and all of us to repentance which will lead to the forgiveness of sins. John is the incarnation of the words of the prophet, Isaiah. John will not let the Herods of the world rest! He challenges, he confronts evil and demands people to change sinful ways. Like his Cousin, Jesus, he has absolutely no use for the sin of hypocrisy. Calling the crowds a "brood of vipers" because they saw his baptism as a simple way to flee God's wrath, he demands that they give some evidence that they really mean to reform their lives! He "shoots down" their argument that simply because they are Abraham's children they "automatically" win a reprieve from God's vengeance. He humiliates them saying that God can raise up children from stones and warns them that God will soon come! (Luke 3:7-10).

When asked what they must do in order to win salvation, John demands that they give away to the poor and the needy half of what they own. He demands that fairness and justice be the rule of life for one and all. He insists that people be treated with what today would be called human dignity! (Luke 3:10-14). His words burned deeply into the hearts of the people because he spoke with God's voice! His words carried God's Word; his lifestyle was radical and detached! He knew as well who he was: "I am baptizing you in water, but there is One to come (he speaks of the Messiah) who is mightier than I. I am not fit to loosen His sandal strap. He will baptize you in the Holy Spirit and in fire. His winnowing-fan is in His hand to clear His threshing floor and gather the wheat into His granary; but the chaff He will burn in unquenchable fire." (Luke: 3:16-17).

John is honesty personified! He is the essence of courage and humility. John is clearly the Prophet of the Near, the Proximate, the very Close. His teachings and lifestyle are needed today more than ever before. We need to follow him closely in order to find Jesus. We need to see John and his message in the words and deeds of Jesus.

From the moment the two unborn babies met, they recognized one another. Later, as an adult, Jesus presented Himself for John's baptism. Suddenly, the skies opened and the Holy Spirit, descending on Jesus in visible form, a dove, carried the Eternal Father's message: "You are My beloved Son. On You My favor rests." (Luke 3:22).

Jesus defended John and John's message by saying simply: "God's wisdom is vindicated by all who accept it." (Luke 7:35). Mark tells us of how John the Baptist died: In his gospel, Mark sees Herod getting lustfully drunk and in this pride-filled impure spirit, having John beheaded! (Mark 6:14-29). Once again, John's words and actions are wedded closer than two pieces of wax melted into one; closer to each other than is the droplet of water to the wine in the chalice as it is offered to God. John is, in a true sense, like his far greater Cousin, the great Lamb of God, a lamb of God. His blood is spilled on the altar of God's integrity and His providence. John died for confronting Herod's sinfulness. John gave his life so that the witness of God's law might prevail.

For His part, Jesus was deeply touched by John's murder. Immediately He and His disciples went on retreat (Mark 6:30,31). This incident would always have a profound impact on Christ. He needs to be with His Father in heaven so that He could comprehend the event of John the Baptist, his life and death. John's strength of character and word both taught and encouraged Christ. Just as John would never compromise God's Word, so God's Word would never sell-out His most excellent Voice! Jesus stood by John as John stood by Jesus.

The relationship between Jesus and John is not only one of physical reality. It is before all else the relationship between two men who knew and respected each other's role in this redemption drama! Again and again Jesus would caution His apostles to "put trust in God." (Mark 11:22). John always did this. It was the all consuming song of his entire life. Wherever he went and whom-so-ever he met, John cried and lived trust in God!

Perhaps this is the greatest lesson John teaches us: to trust in the providence of Almighty God! God is the Creator. God is the Redeemer. God is the Sanctifier. God is our destiny but He is far more. He is our Father. Not even John could imagine how close God is to us. He sees the Messiah and finds the God of Abraham, Isaac and Jacob! He is called the greatest among us born of women; yet, John's greatness is limited: did not Jesus clearly say: " ... the least born into the Kingdom of God is greater than (even) John the Baptist." (Matthew 11:1). He called the Baptist, Elijah (Matthew 11 :14) and demands that we heed carefully what John teaches!

Jesus, John and "me": the trilogy that brings God to the world and the world to God, that is if the "me," i. e., you and I, are bold and brave enough to become like Jesus and John! Are we willing to put ourselves and our own comfort levels at risk to have that mind in us that is in the Word and the Voice? Are we willing to become like them who physically resemble you and me? Are we willing to die, to give our lives as they did for us? The decision, in the final analysis, will determine if we will live forever with them in their home or go to some other place we could never call "home!"

THE UNSPOKEN – THE HIDDEN

" ... He descended into hell, the third day
He rose from the dead ...." (Apostles' Creed)

There were so very many souls! They were at rest but not really at peace. There was tranquility but still a quiet restlessness as they awaited the redemption of the eternal Israel, the rebirth into eternal life of the nation!

The two of them were truly soul-mates. They enjoyed each other and loved telling the countless good souls of the wonders of God's love. Even the prophets listened to them! Of all those who died awaiting the justice of their good deeds these two were the very first, the very best.

The one spoke: "I remember when I first learned of her pregnancy. I was heartbroken! I couldn't believe that she would, let alone could have, done that! The law required her to be put to death but I couldn't do that! She was so beautiful, so pure and innocent – but how could she do such a thing? Never, never did I think there would be another answer. It took all I had to suspend my belief that the law had to be followed! I had made arrangements to have her live in another village with a change of name. Then it happened: I had a startling dream. I awakened in a cold sweat and remembered Joseph of old, my namesake. He was a dreamer as well. Look what he accomplished by following his dreams. But my dream was so very, very real! The voice was gentle, strong and so very convincing. I really didn't understand when the voice told me that the unborn baby was destined to be the "Promised" of Israel, begotten by "God's own Spirit."

The other spoke: "Yes, I too had to follow my own dreams. Before my birth I heard that voice telling me that

God's Word would be carried on my voice as He lived in my heart! Surely, there were many voices which carried God's Word to Israel – why my voice and why a 'singular Word'? What did it mean? I studied the sacred books and experienced in the deepest core of my being the goodness of God. I fell hopelessly in love with Him! I couldn't stand to see people reject His message, pretending to be something other than what all of us truly are, absolute sinners! I wanted to serve Him. Then I saw heaven open and God's love coming upon the Son of your dear wife! I never knew Him when we were children. I hardly recognized Him at the Jordan River – but He was different: His looks; His bearing; His speech all reflected what I knew – somehow – to be God's love!

"I tried to be sure. I sent messengers, my followers, to ask Him if He was the Messiah. He simply told them to look at the signs He performed, the works He did. I had expected a definite 'yes' or 'no.' But the more I thought about it, the more aware I am that I had to open my eyes, my God-given eyes, mind and sensitivity to ponder within myself, to get in touch with my own spirit so that I could determine from His actions and words if He truly was the Messiah or not! I had the greatest gift of knowing, of believing that He is truly God's Son. One day, we shall see Him again. I'm sure of it!"

They spoke to each other, the old father and young prophet, in such a way that others could overhear their words. Their conversation flowed and helped to greatly ease the anticipation of waiting. Years, centuries of waiting.

A quiet voice, a third Person, spoke: "But He had to live this way and even to suffer and die so that God's glory could be celebrated in the brightness and goodness of people who truly loved God in the only way they knew." The newcomer was gentle, as was seen in the in the manner of His composure and speech. He too was different. He hadn't been noticed before. Usually people who arrived late were at the rear of the line. "He was a man, yes; but remember, only God could forgive sins; only God could open the barriers which blocked humanity from the Kingdom of God." The new arrival understood the Scripture. Could He have seen the prophet from Nazareth? What happened to Jesus, the son of Joseph and Mary?

A quiet fell over the assembly; it wasn't noticed at first but something must have happened. People were all focused, all listening. It wasn't easy to see the newcomer's face as the cloak's headpiece covered His brow. Then the obvious spoke eloquently: this newcomer's body was different. Unlike the bodies of the just who died, returning to the dust from which they were made, His body glowed, it radiated!

The old man spoke: "I think I've heard that voice before."

"I too think I've heard it," thought the Baptist.

The newcomer was near the old man. Could that be tears? "How could that be tears?" he thought. "I don't have my body! But it feels like tears! I'm so happy. I feel light, sort of floating! The closer I get to Him the better I feel! I wonder if I could get a closer look, only a little closer look ...!

The newcomer uncovered His face. The old man gazed a penetrating stare of recognition. The newcomer spoke softly "Abba, my Daddy, it is I ... do not be afraid!" Joseph, speechless and cold suddenly found himself, arms wide-opened throwing himself around his Jesus, his boy, the step-son he had raised. 'My God, my all, it is you, my Jesus ... Your mother, my dearest love, how is she?" The Messiah smiled as the totality of the souls sang in that heavenly joy the song of the angels of Bethlehem: "Glory to God in the highest ... Blessed, blessed is He, the Messiah, the Redeemer who comes to bring us into heaven, into the Father's arms! Hosanna, Hosanna in the highest!"

Suddenly, the choirs of angels joined in the great hymn of God's glory. Before all, one with the Father and Holy Spirit the fullness of Divinity bursting forth from the risen body of their step-Son and Cousin, the Lord Jesus Christ, Joseph and John knew why they lived as they did! There were no other choices save to do God's will: for Joseph to raise Him caring for Him, teaching Him; for John, announcing Him and dying for Him.

This moment of eternity; this greatest of salvation's events now cleared all confusion's clouds. The real sun is the Son of God! Jesus is the Christ, God's way of creating a greater garden than Eden could ever have been or could ever be! Jesus Christ is heaven! He is the new Order, the perfect blending of Creator and creation. From now on men would know God and God would never reject humanity! From henceforth, now and forever, the gates of heaven would be opened for those who "die in the Lord."

Joseph the carpenter and John the Baptist would never know sorrow again! The Master's touch would remove the sting of loss, of death without God. The Lord would never let anything happen to His love, His own. Jesus, the newly risen, had – as the Apostles' Creed says – "(He) descended into hell" – this waiting place, not the "hell" of the damned but the "hell" of the first who died before Calvary's greatest Martyr and who were waiting, anticipating this moment! Jesus had opened heaven's gates. From now on Joseph would be called Saint and the Baptist would ever be called truly holy! Gone forever was the "hell of the just." The seed instantly became the flower of eternity; the night became the day and God and the saints were forever one! Amen!

CONTEMPLATION – PRAYER

Good St. Joseph, holy John the Baptist – no doubt you had met during your earthly lives. No doubt you spent wonderful moments together awaiting the redemption of your people. Yet how differently you died. You, Joseph, in the arms of your Mary and her Son; you, John, thrown upon the executioner's block by people who hated you! Both lovers, both strong and good men, both incarnations of God's will!

From you, Joseph, I learn quiet reflection and comforting, loving thoughts. Again and again you are called, during your early life, to believe in the incredible so you can do the impossible: A little girl conceives by God, God's Divine Son; Kings visit from the East while a mad ruler seeks to kill life itself, the King of Kings and Lord of Lords. You, Joseph, must make sense out of all of this; you must bring peace out of rage and love out of a king's hatred. From you, I learn to trust God's ways. From your pure love, I learn how to love purely! From you I experience the touch of Jesus and the caress of Mary. For you are the patron of a happy death. Let me die in your arms. Help me to enter heaven with my loved ones to welcome me and introduce me to Jesus and Mary as you so quietly and gently introduced them with great dignity and, thanks to you, with a safe reputation, to the people of your village.

What a man you must have been: quiet, ever so kind, never judgmental or brooding; always open, welcoming and caring. O greatest of Protectors, O kindest of Guardians, help me to live so that if I die, a heart-beat from now, in the presence of Nazareth's Holy Family, I may soon be one with my family and your Family forever!

And you, Saint John the Baptist, what must your life, your childhood and adulthood have been like? Your parents were so very old. It would seem that you had to bury them both before you went into the desert. How you must have grieved for them! I can imagine how deeply they loved you and lived for you. You were their dream come true! No doubt they poured their love upon you, giving you all they had and even what they didn't have. Unspoiled, you loved and cared for them! Did Elizabeth, your dear mother, die in your arms? Did your dearest Dad bury her as a priest of the ancient covenant? When did you experience the loss of your family, O blessed St. John the Baptist?

Life seems to be one loss after another! Is heaven that place where we shall never hear the words "good bye" again? If heaven really is that eternal moment, that blissful event, help us, dear St. John the Baptist, to experience your joy at seeing again your own dear parents and your Jesus! Help us to take the chances and the risks we need to make in order to challenge ourselves, and all those whose paths cross ours, to live the Gospel values taught by Jesus! Give us the courage to challenge and strengthen our sisters and brothers in the faith of the Church. Keep us faithful to our words and honest in our deeds. Shelter us from the cries of the dishonest and the lies of the worldly. Let us place our faith in the God who transforms the seed into the flower and the darkest night into the brightest day. Help us to trust in God and in His way rather than in our own very limited and selfish ways! Help us, John, to be totally God's son/daughter! Help us to be unafraid of those who would make the needs of the body the first call on our priorities! Help us to deny our bodies so as to affirm our minds and spirits. Ask God to let His Spirit control our human spirits and minds so that our bodies will truly reflect that Divinity living ever in Jesus and because of Him, living always in us. Amen!

HIS WILL IN MY LIFE

I resolve to pray daily for the courage to challenge myself to live the Gospel values so clearly lived by Joseph and by John the Baptist. I promise that as Joseph and John the Baptist, both of whom died before the Lord's resurrection, lived totally abandoned to God and trusting in God and the Messiah, so I shall live letting God be God in my life.

I promise that like John and Joseph, I shall be focused and pure in thought, word and deed. I shall try to practice spending at least one hour every day in prayer. This will include examining my conscience in the light of the wishes of Jesus for me. I resolve to make good use of the sacrament of reconciliation knowing that the mercy of God is all restoring, all renewing.

I firmly pledge to spend time in the hiddenness of "God's quiet" thinking about Jesus, John the Baptist and Joseph and how they must have spoken to each other. What must their relationship have been like? How can I learn to better use my time to get to know John and Joseph better, these two men whose lives so deeply impacted that of Jesus Christ! What can they tell me about Jesus? What virtues did they have that He, the Messiah, loved so deeply?

I pray that like Joseph I will die in the arms of Jesus and Mary. I hope that like John the Baptist I will be ready to face the most horrible of deaths if God so desires. Whatever be God's will, may His kingdom come here on earth and in me now so that for all eternity I may pray: yes, maranatha! Come, Lord Jesus! Amen!

CHAPTER THREE

THE TEMPTATIONS OF JESUS
AS HE BEGINS HIS PUBLIC MINISTRY:
AM I INVOLVED?
IF SO, TO WHAT DEGREE
DOES THIS APPLY TO MY LIFE?

"Then Jesus was led into the desert by the Spirit to be tempted by the devil. He spent forty days and forty nights, and afterward (He) was hungry. The tempter approached and said to Him, 'If you are the Son of God, command these stones to turn to bread.' Jesus replied, 'Scripture has it: not on bread alone is man to live but on every utterance that comes from the mouth of God.'"

Next the devil took Him to the holy city (Jerusalem), set Him on the parapet of the temple, and said, 'If You are the Son of God, throw Yourself down, Scripture has it: 'He will bid His angels take care of you; with their hands they will support You that You may never stumble on a stone.' Jesus answered him, 'Scripture has it: You shall not put the Lord your God to the test.'"

Then the devil took Him up a very high mountain and displayed before Him all the kingdoms of the world in their magnificence, promising, 'All these will I bestow on you if You prostrate Yourself in homage before me.' At this, Jesus said to him, "Away with you, Satan! Scripture has it: 'You shall do homage to the Lord your God; Him alone shall you adore.' At that the devil left Him, and angels came and waited on Him." (Matt. 4:1-11).

Like us in all things but sin, the Lord Jesus Christ experienced temptations against the body, the mind and the spirit! The body places us in touch with the physical world, the world of "feeling," the material. The mind (soul) places us in touch with the world of ideas, the whole world of thought. The spirit puts us in touch with the transcendental, the eternal! Jesus experienced temptations against all of these "worlds." Satan knew He was tired; Satan knew He was hungry; mind-weary and heavy in spirit. Jesus had suffered from the full awareness of the task entrusted to Him by the Father. Redeemer of the world, He was about to begin His work. He saw the future clearly!

Can we imagine the amount of apprehension He must have experienced going through these days of retreat? For us today, if we do make a retreat, we go to a comfortable retreat house, we are served good meals and sleep on fine mattresses in climate controlled rooms! The desert was totally unlike this! All Jesus had were the clothes on His back. He had to fend for Himself. No doubt He ate the fare of the desert, locust and wild honey. Water was scarce and danger was everywhere! It was being alone and that loneliness which made the retreat nearly impossible! Jesus knew from the very start how much He would need to depend upon His Father! Sinless Himself as a victim for sinners, He was aware that in and of Himself, as man, He would need to throw Himself on the Father's mercy.

The coldness of desert nights matched in extremes the heat of day in this wilderness. It would seem that if all a person, caught-up in this environment, had to do was to survive – that was enough! Jesus, confronted with the ultimate reality of His destiny, faced the future and lived in the now!

He knew that many would call Him Lord, Teacher and Master but there would be so very, very few who, in the final analysis would "be there" when all the chips were down! On Calvary, there would be few, so very, very few, to look upon Him with love and there would be hardly anyone who would understand the gift He was to make of His life and witness so that the world might be redeemed and the new creation come into being! Jesus, knowing that the tasks of the next three years of public ministry would literally be back-breaking and totally consuming, faced even the risk of temptation for our sakes! He would know the evils of Satan face-to-face. He would confront the demon and win because His great heart was totally grounded in the Father! He wanted to know and even to feel the coldness and cunningness of the devil. That's why He was tempted!

I believe He needed to experience this in order to find a way to excuse us when we sin, as we are so much weaker than our Messiah! He really, for our sakes, needed to experience rejection. That's why He was born in a stable and not Bethlehem's inn. He needed to know what the homeless experienced. That's why foxes have dens and birds have nests but He had no place to lay His head. He felt it necessary to be cold and hot and experience these natural extremes with nothing to brace Him against either so that we could never say He wouldn't know our pain!

Jesus Christ is truly human. His body, mind and Divine Spirit reacted to the harsh realities of nature as do we.

As man, He wanted to feel, to know and to understand our own condition. That's why He constantly drifted toward the rejected among us: the poor, the vulnerable elderly, the lepers and sick, the physically scarred and psychologically crippled were among His greatest loves. Jesus truly experienced every kind of hurt known to us. Made in our image and likeness, as man, He found a way to save us despite ourselves! Jesus knew that – because they choose it – the Blessed Trinity would insist that people, redeemed people, had to share in the life of God. God, therefore, had to suffer in His human nature! Jesus is a Divine Person, He is the Eternal Son, the Word of God; however, He possesses, in addition to the Divine Nature of the Godhead, a human nature like ours! He has a human body and a human soul. Both are held in existence by the Second Person of the Blessed Trinity, the Word of God. Jesus Christ, as a Person, is God! Jesus Christ as man has a human nature. "Person" answers the question "Who?" "Nature" answers the question "What?" In His human nature, Christ experienced our every temptation even to the point of total depression: "My God, My God, why have You forsaken Me?" He was totally rejected! He felt it!

Driven out of Bethlehem, Nazareth, Jerusalem and unwelcome in many of the other territories, He refused to surrender to Satan's ways! He simply would not give in to the evil that wanted Him to have all the kingdoms of the world if only He, the Son of God, the Creator would kneel to the creature, Satan!

From time immemorial, the struggle between good and evil has always involved the highest of God's creation. The angels rebelled against the Creator. So beautiful, so magnificent were they (the choirs of angels) that, so we are told, some of them thought they could challenge the Creator and win! Their pride drew them away from God. They instantaneously thought themselves better than God and openly rebelled. The truly good among their numbers felt themselves strengthened by God to fight for God, for truth! The creature is never equal with the Creator! Common sense tells us that, yet, these few lacked all common sense. Driven out of heaven, they would forever seek to disrupt God's design for His creatures, especially the highest of His creatures in the order of rational life, the choirs of angels. From before time, in that place where angels live, creatures have given into temptation! Like us, so too were the angels given free will, that ability to say "yes" or "no" to God's will.

Today, especially, we hear of "freedom" confused with "license"! Freedom, true freedom, has everything to do with what philosophers call the "final cause," the reason why we are made. Why were we made? To know completely, to love totally, and serve fully the Creator while we live here on earth and hence if we do this, to experience His life fully in heaven! Hence, true freedom is the fulfillment totally of

God's will for me. That is why the various helps God gives us along the way of life never inhibits or impedes our freedom. "Grace," as these helps are called, always makes the exercise of free will more fully complete, more totally perfect as the Creator sees it.

If I make a pie, the final cause of the pie is to be eaten, to be enjoyed! The pie cannot be put on a shelf without it eventually decaying or being consumed. It may be temporarily used as a decoration, but ultimately it must be eaten for it to fulfill its final cause, its purpose, the reason for its having been made!

Our final cause, our destiny, is to fulfill the Creator's plan for us. This we must do! Jesus' final cause was to glorify the Father by redeeming the fallen broken creation called, humanity. When we are tempted, as when He was tempted, He and we know so very well that what appears to be a stumbling block to destiny is really meant to be a stepping stone to heaven!

Temptations are a part of all of our lives. They are the fire that proves the mettle; they are the steps leading to our full incorporation into Christ's human nature which is one with the Divine Creator whose life we will share!

THE UNSPOKEN – THE HIDDEN

"Jesus toured all of Galilee. He taught in their synagogues, proclaimed the good news of the kingdom, and cured the people of every disease and illness. As a consequence of this, His reputation traveled the length of Syria. They carried to Him all those afflicted with various diseases and racked with pain: the possessed, the lunatics, the paralyzed. He cured them all. The great crowds that followed Him came from Galilee, the Ten Cities, Jerusalem and Judea, and from across the Jordan." (Matt. 4:23-25).

The Master thought: "Lord, My Father, there are so very many of them! So many sick, so many mentally disturbed, so many with countless needs! Lord God, what am I to do? If I tell them what they cannot understand, I will be responsible for them leaving. But I must tell them. I simply can't go on curing the sick while ignoring the message of why I came! You sent Me that they may have life and have it to the fullest! I came to prepare Our home for them so that where We are, they may likewise be! I will tell them what I am all about! I will tell them how they must live. (Matt. 5:1-12); I will explain to them how they can become good disciples (Matt 5:13-16) and how the old and new laws relate to each other (Matt. 5:17-48; 6:1-33; 7:1-27). Then they will understand!"

The crowds listened spellbound to the teaching of the Master. Did they hear? Did they hear and understand? Did they put His teaching into action? No doubt He was exhausted by the teaching. He prayed they would understand the full dimension of His teachings. He had not come to simply cure physical illnesses. He came specifically to bring the kingdom of God to the earth. Would they really understand?

Almost immediately, a leper showed up. He fell at the

feet of Jesus and begged the Lord to cure him. Immediately, Jesus responded: "I do will it (to cure you). Be cured." (Matt. 8:3b). Perhaps it was at this moment that Jesus realized they did not understand who He was, why He had come and the whole purpose of His mission! Why else would He have said to the leper: "See to it that you tell no one. Go and show yourself to the priest and offer the gift Moses prescribed. That should be the proof they need." (Matt. 8:4).

Following the Scriptures we see the many miracles the Lord performed: the Centurion's servant (Matt. 8:5-13); Peter's mother-in-law (Matt. 8:14); countless exorcisms (Matt. 8:26); protecting His disciples from the violence of nature (Matt. 8:23-27). Still they didn't understand!

How must He have felt? Most of us can imagine the profound discouragement, perhaps even the justified anger, He had every right to feel! Still the people came, more and more and in greater and greater numbers: the paralytic at Capernaum; the dead girl, daughter of the synagogue leader; the two blind men and possessed mute; they came and kept coming. Surely they would listen to Him as He spoke about the Father and the Kingdom He was preparing for the true disciples beyond the grave, that Kingdom which we call heaven! Surely they would listen and hear!

How did Jesus respond to this personal defeat? How did He react to the ceaseless cries of the people whose attention, whose needs, were focused solely on the relief from physical problems? He had told them and us that He did not come simply to cure the bodies' pains. He came to bring eternal life to all of us!

The just anger seemingly grew within Him. The leaders came up to Him again and again to challenge Him. Witness the pride-filled arrogance of the Pharisees who spied His disciples pulling off the heads of grain and eating them on the

Sabbath (Matt. 12:1-2). His response was one of mercy but would soon change! He cures the man whose hand was shriveled and continues to show mercy while warning all of His followers sternly and ordering them not to make public what He had done! The tension was mounting, the justified anger about to boil over! The concrete blindness of the Pharisees and their demeanor and obvious hatred for God's truth finally did it! He blew!: "I assure you, on judgment day people will be held accountable for every unguarded word they speak. By your own words you will be acquitted and by your words you will be condemned!" (Matt. 12:36-37).

The weight He carried and the disappointment of Jesus Christ must have known no relief! In (his) prologue, the writer of the Gospel of John says clearly: " ... To His own He came, yet His own did not accept Him ..." (John 1:11). Rejection followed Him from the beginning. What level of temptation to despair must this have been? How often was He challenged to throw in the towel? He not only suffered from physical discomfort as He was continually on the road, He was also attacked in the very core of His being by the hostile actions, spoken of and taken, against His gospel, His message! Even His parables were thought to be unacceptable! Those who knew Him best, the closest disciples, asked Him to explain in plain language, the parables (Matt. 13:36). Temptations to discouragement were His constant companions. Continually, He had to explain Himself. Not because they didn't or couldn't understand, but because they wouldn't take the time or invest the energy to understand!

How often He wanted to engage them in fruitful discussions, but they hadn't really listened with understanding hearts and pondering minds. Unlike Mary who listened, who pondered, these guys were almost incapable of hearing because of their all-embracing selfishness! Temptations to give-up trying must have enveloped His mind each time He tried falling asleep. Temptations to lash out and ask His Father for 12 (or more) legions of angels (6,000 in a Roman legion) to destroy this self-centered bunch of ignorant people must have been always a spoken word and a moment away! After all, look at what happened to the people of Israel in the Old Testament due to their own hardness of heart! The entire book of Exodus speaks of God's disappointment and His justified anger! Did the eternal Son of God, equal with the Father, not have an equal right to express His own anger? I think so!

Still, He fed the hungry – 4,000 men, not including women and children (Matt. 15:38). But there is a change coming as surely as the color of the sky foretells the quality of the day (Matt. 16:1-4). He begins to speak openly and directly about their sins. He talks of their evil "yeast." (Matt. 16:5-12). He seems to feel He had done all He was capable of doing. He begins to prepare for the end! He does not despair, rather, He prepares for His own passover and continues to perform those constant requests for cures from physical ills. He speaks of prayer but lives distantly and, at times, alone! He tries to explain again what must be done to inherit eternal life and finally, He tells them that He is going up to Jerusalem to be delivered over to evil men and to give up His life.

In the Temple He tells His disciples to obey the orders of the Scribes and Pharisees while not following their example. (Matt. 23:2-3). Angry because He was totally unable to break through their hypocrisy, He finally exploded and told them and all in their hearing, exactly what He thought (cf. Matt. 12:1-39)! In this lengthy passage, Jesus tells us about evil and how evil gets possession of us! The Scribes and Pharisees are broods of vipers who are thoroughly evil to the very core of their beings!

CONTEMPLATION – PRAYER

Jesus, born into sinful humanity, Innocence Itself, You introduced a new dimension to the word for love: agapè! The love that led You, Eternal Word and Second Person of the Most Blessed Trinity, to leave the eternal comfort of heaven in order to enter the fallen human condition so that a new world, a new creation may begin, saw You lower Yourself to become our Bread of Life and our Cup of Eternal Salvation.

You found a way to be tempted, exposing Yourself to all the evil in this lost paradise! You took upon Yourself our pain, our anxiety, our stress. You literally became all pain so that we could never say You didn't understand us. Born in rejection, You grew up in poverty and spoke in painful ways to a people who didn't even listen, about a kingdom beyond the grave but possible even now of achieving if only we would listen, hear and act!

How could we ever complain again as we see a crucifix and examine Your thorn-crowned head, nail-pierced hands, and spiked feet? How could we ever say that our hearts were broken when disappointment came our way? Your pierced heart, which held all the secrets of love's deepest ways, was pulled apart for us. All Your precious blood was shed for us even to the point where nothing was left save a few drops of water.

Your life was totally positive. The negative never managed to overcome You. The world, the flesh and the devil threw their best punches Your way and still You reached deeply within Yourself to the heart of Your Godhead and repelled all evil! You gave us a perfect example that as You did so we must do in like manner.

You teach us that temptation in life is like fire in metal.

The refiner takes the stones containing the precious metal and the heat of the fire burns away the lesser elements leaving only the pure gold! Temptation tests our moral mettle and makes us stronger if we resist! You taught us, dear Lord, to resist and to send the devil, source of all evil, back into the fires of hell!

When we want to give into ourselves and make ourselves feel we are justified, we need only to look at Your life to find a motive to die to ourselves so we might live with You, in You and for You!

Lord, when we stop to consider what the Holy Eucharist, the Blessed Sacrament, is supposed to do for us, we are truly humbled! As, through the bio-chemical process of metabolism, i.e., digestion, food becomes a part of our body and blood, so when we receive You in the Blessed Eucharist, we become a part of You! Heaven comes to earth and the Kingdom of God is within us! The opposite of digestion takes place: You ingest us! You become one with us! Lord, truly heaven is here; heaven is now; heaven is within us when we receive Holy Communion; we, Lord, become You!

God is imprisoned under the elements of bread and wine, literally our food and drink, come solely to change us into Himself. What is heaven if not Holy Communion? When we stop to realize the gift of the Blessed Sacrament and its true purpose, to make heaven come right here and now, we should never be sad again.

We can pray:
"Jesus, heart of love, mind of the Father,
Speak to my mind, embrace Thou my heart.
Let me live, not I, but You living
within my essence, my being.
Jesus, be closer to me than the air
in my lungs; the blood in my arteries!

Jesus, change me, transfigure me into
Your image and Your likeness!
Jesus, never let temptation possess me
to the point of compromising my salvation.
Jesus, test me, but protect me! Help me
to resist all temptation and to choose
all things that You approve!
Jesus, bless my relationships. Strengthen
those that are healthy and rid me of
those that are sinful and impure.
Jesus, help me to live on this earth,
fully conscious that I am but a heart-beat
away from death. Help me to work each day
as if I would live forever!
Jesus, help me to live as if I would die today!
Amen!

HIS WILL IN MY LIFE

I resolve to resist all temptation by praying, the moment the temptation comes: "God my Father, in the Name of Jesus, my brother and Lord, sustain me in Your peace and Your serenity!"

I promise to make use of the sacrament of reconciliation (confession) in order to dispose myself to grow in grace. I promise to examine my conscience in the light of the way of Jesus Christ and to confront myself with the whole and true Christ before I dare to accept the comforts of His Gospel.

I firmly pledge to meditate on the Blessed Eucharist and to be in the Divine Presence, saying nothing but simply contemplating the Word of God always waiting for me! I promise to live in thanksgiving for my redemption and never to become discouraged as I live my life in Jesus and Mary.

Finally, I pray that Jesus and Mary shield me from temptation to sin and that should I sin, they assist me to reconcile myself to God's love by taking advantage of sacramental confession and of avoiding discouragement and depression since, though a sinner, I am still worth the blood of Christ.

Amen!

CHAPTER FOUR

THE MIRACLES OF JESUS: CAN I EXPECT ONE TODAY? IF SO, WHAT DO I HAVE TO DO TO GET A MIRACLE FOR MYSELF?

He taught by preaching, living according to His Father's will and by His compassion! Compassion for the Centurion's servant (Luke 7:1-10); the widow's son (Luke 7:11-17); the penitent woman (Luke 7:36-48); Jairus' child, a hemorrhage victim (Luke 8:40-56); and so many, many others. Miracle after miracle was performed to cure the sick among the people of His day. Despite this, it is obvious that He began to "resent" having to perform miracles. It seemed they "got in the way" of His preaching and teaching! He was absolutely focused on "clearing up" the "popular notions" of the coming Messiah!

Three elements seem to converge at this time: He preaches, clarifies and reveals the proper face of His Father; He performs miracles to demonstrate His mandate from God; He gives us the real test of discipleship. It is this "real test of discipleship," that is submission to God's will, we do need to stress for ourselves and all of us who live in our western culture!

We look to the 14th chapter of John's gospel to see His mission with reference to His disciples and His relationship to Almighty God. Clearer than in any other piece of Scripture, we hear Him distinctly and clearly say: "Do not let your hearts be troubled. Have faith in God and faith in Me. In My Father's house there are many dwelling places; otherwise, how could I have told you that I go (was going) to prepare a place for you? I am indeed going to prepare a place for you and then I shall come back to take you with Me, that where I am you also may be. You know the way that leads where I go." "Lord," said Thomas, "we do not know where You are going. How can we know the way?" Jesus told him: "I am the way, and the truth, and the life; no one comes to the Father but through Me. If you really knew Me, you would know My Father also. From this point on you know Him; you have seen Him." "Lord," Philip said to Him, "show us the Father and that will be enough for us." "Philip," Jesus replied, "after I have been with you all this time, you still do not know Me?"

"Whoever has seen Me has seen the Father ...
Do you not believe that I am in the Father
and the Father is in Me?" (John 14:1-10).

The 14th chapter continues, and when we meditate on faith in this light and that of the last things, that is to say, our preparation for death, our rendering an accounting to God of how well we have kept His law (submission to God's will) and invested our God given talents, we will then know if we have that quality of faith so necessary to get a miracle. Truly, we need to spend time with our Bible in hand. This time, I suggest, can best be kept before the Blessed Sacrament or in a special corner of our homes we reserve for prayer.

In John 15, we hear clearly the cry of the Lord to His disciples: "If you find that the world hates you, know it hated Me before you. If you belonged to the world, it (the world) would love you as its own; the reason it hates you is that you do not belong to the world. But I chose you out of the world. Remember what I told you: no slave is greater than his master. They will harry you as they harried Me. They will respect your words as much as they respected Mine. All this they will do to you because of My Name, for they know nothing of Him who sent Me. If I had not come to them and spoken to them, they would not be guilty of sin; now, however, their sin cannot be excused. To hate Me is to hate My Father ...(quoting the ancient law, Jesus concludes), They hated Me without cause." (John 15:16-23; 25b).

Jesus truly suffered in the deepest dimensions of His

soul! He simply couldn't make them (the worldly) hear and ponder what He was doing and saying. Filled with themselves, people of the world, worldly people, never hear Christ, never pay Him more than a very passing glance! In a car, as we drive or ride along, we pass countless buildings, signs, automobiles, construction sites, etc., etc. Never, never do we pay them more than a passing glance. The "worldly" quality in each of us does that! It makes us lose focus! It becomes almost impossible for us to live the caution of Jesus to His disciples, His closest followers: "Live on in My love." (John 15:9b). We also forget His introduction to this great command: "As the Father has loved Me, so I have loved you." (John 15:9a).

To "live on in the love" of Jesus Christ means simply to stay focused on Christ. We constantly have our focus "messed up" by worldly allurements and body or appetite needs! Think of what Jesus said: "As the Father has loved Me, so I have loved you." As the Father loves the Son, in the same way and in the same manner as the Father loves Jesus, so Jesus, the Eternal Word, the Eternal God, loves each of us! Wow!

What else could have seen Him pick up that cross on the road to Calvary. What else, other than love, the agapè love, could have seen Him stick with us: fickle, unlovable, proud, arrogant and out-and-out hateful types that we are! I think we need to review again and again these passages from the 15th Chapter of John.

Called by Jesus to be His special followers, we absolutely need to stay close to Him. We need to fight against evil and know that we will never win the battle, let alone the war, unless we love – or try to love – as Jesus loves!

St. Paul never founded a Church in Athens! Do you know why? Read Acts 17. In the Areopagus, the "town center" where the "unto the manor-born" wealthy and intellectuals gathered to debate as if they were gods, Paul attempted to tell them of Jesus. His discourse, excellent prose and insightful poetry, I'm sure, found him unable to preach about "Christ and Him crucified"! He found a statue (among the dozens of equally sized statues) marked "To a God Unknown." Paul then said that the "God Unknown" was the Father of Jesus. Paul failed to tie the whole thing together so that when he spoke of the "raising of the dead" they shut their ears and turned him off (the way we turn off the television or car radio)! They turned away!

Paul walked all the way back to Corinth where he founded a Church and wrote his most challenging letter. Read the First Letter to the Corinthians! It contains all the information – practical information on how to really be a faithfilled follower (disciple) of Jesus Christ! Perhaps a particular family or group or parish may be experiencing problems. If so, I suggest a group meeting or even a series of meetings where the First Letter to the Corinthians might be read – in all of its parts – reflected upon and talked about in the light of those problems the group may be experiencing. I guarantee that the difficulty or problem will be resolved if the instructions given by Paul in this great epistle would be followed.

Paul loved like Jesus. But Paul's love, like all of us when we attempt to love, had to mature.

Paul learned a lesson in Athens. Maybe he learned many lessons, but one thing is certain: that experience changed Paul! It made him look at how he loved Jesus. It tied his discussion of love found in 1 Corinthians 13:1-13, perhaps the most quoted passage in the whole Bible, into the way in which the Father loves the Son (Jesus) and in which Jesus loves us. It is the way we must love one another!

"Now I will show you the way which surpasses all the others.

If I speak with human tongues and angelic as well, but do not have love, I am a noisy gong, a clanging cymbal.

If I have the gift of prophecy and, with full knowledge, comprehend all mysteries,
if I have faith great enough to move mountains, but have not love, I am nothing.

If I give everything I have to feed the poor and hand over my body to be burned, but have not love, I gain nothing.

Love is patient, love is kind. Love is not jealous, it does not put on airs, it is not snobbish. Love is never rude, it is not self-seeking, it is not prone to anger; neither does it brood over injuries.

Love does not rejoice in what is wrong but rejoices with the truth.

There is no limit to love's forbearance, to its trust, its hope, its power to endure.

Love never fails. Prophecies will cease, tongues will be silent, knowledge will pass away ... There are in the end three things that last: faith, hope, and love, and the greatest of these is love."

(1 Cor. 13:1-8; 13.)

In the first epistle of John, chapter 4 verses 16b-18, we complete the reason why Paul wrote and lived as he did and we find, as well, the answer to whatever questions we may still have on this word we call "love." John writes: "God is love, and he who abides (lives) in love abides in God, and God in him." Furthermore, the author of the same epistle teaches: "We for our part, love because He (Christ Jesus, our

Lord and God) first loved us." (1 John 4:19).

Paul, in love with Christ and living within His Christ-given love, spends his whole life as Christ's apostle teaching and proclaiming the words of John 5:1-5: "Everyone who believes that Jesus is the Christ has been begotten of God. Now, everyone who loves the Father loves the child (Jesus) He has begotten. We can be sure that we love God's children when we love God and do what He has commanded. The love of God consists in this: that we keep His commandments – and His commandments are not burdensome. Everyone begotten of God conquers the world, and the power that has conquered the world is this faith of ours. Who, then is conqueror of the world? The one who believes that Jesus is the Son of God."

This is where we must answer the question which begins this chapter: Can I expect a miracle today and what do I have to do to get a miracle?

Clearly, it is a miracle of God's providence and His will that the Holy Spirit living inside of us enables us to call Jesus, "Lord." It is a miracle of grace that we have the ability to love as Jesus loves! It is a miracle of faith that we can answer the call of God – if we totally abandon ourselves to a life-style in complete conformity to the challenges of the gospel, we will be disposing ourselves to the world of miracles!

Miracles come when what we ask is directly in agreement with God's revealed truth in Christ Jesus our Lord. Miracles come when we ask after we submit to the will of God. Submission to God's will disposes us to know for what to ask, when to ask, and how to ask! Predisposition to a miracle is essential. If I'm living a life that is not in conformity to God's will, I have no right to expect the Lord to grant my request! On the other hand, if I pray in the selfless way of the Lord and His holy ones, an answer will come and, I believe, that answer will be a miracle!

Bishop Fulton J. Sheen once told me of a prayer that will always be answered! He prayed the prayer himself and it was always answered! The prayer is simply this: "Lord, send me suffering to save a soul." Note the various components to the prayer: (1) It is a totally "other-conscious" prayer which – as Sheen says – is rooted in God's agapè (love). (2) It says (and implies) simply that if it possible to take the blood of a healthy person and transfuse that blood into a sick person (all things being equal), thereby making the sick person better, it should be possible to take the prayer of a healthy redeemed soul and apply it to a sick soul thereby getting the sick soul to recover in the same way as the healthy blood brings healing to the sick person! Makes sense!

Submission to God's will brings about a predisposition to receiving miracles! Miracles of grace and love do happen. We have no call on miracles from God unless we are really one of His Son's redeemed. The person whose happiness rests in doing God's will always finds his/her prayers answered. They know how to pray and how to worship and their devotion, i.e., their total selves, are completely tuned-into how life is lived in God. For them, the kingdom of God is within them and that, in itself, is the greatest and most real miracle.

When asking for a miracle, they ask for, or on behalf of, another! Whatever be God's holy will, they accept it because it is God's will, His choice. They never question it. They have peace and serenity. They know that only one thing is really necessary and that one thing is to save one's soul. They live for God alone and all other loves are found in Him. This is the reason why so many miracles happened in the life of

Mother Teresa of Calcutta, foundress of the Missionaries of Charity. Submission to God's will is the key to obtaining a life of miracles. Read 1 Corinthians 15! This is the essence of Christian teaching on a pre-disposition to getting a miracle. When we die to our selfishness and live in, for and with Christ, we will be a living, breathing miracle of God's love. Paul became a living miracle because he fell in love, real love, with Christ!

THE UNSPOKEN – THE HIDDEN

Lord, You must have gotten tired. There were countless needy. You responded to them yet You longed to go to Your Father's home, to be with Your Father. You would often seek to be alone with God. In the wilderness, up on the top of a mountain or in the valley, You simply wanted and You needed time alone with God, Your Father!

Your faith in the Father was the all important cornerstone of Your human life, of Your preaching ministry. Lord Jesus Christ, You told us to ask and we would receive, seek and we would find, knock and it would be opened for us. (Matt. 7:7).

You made a positive answer to our prayer possible. Possible, yes, and even probable if we knew what to do and how to do it when we asked for what we wanted.

"All this talk of His about going back to the Father, do you understand any of it, Philip?" said Thomas. "The Father!?" exclaimed Philip, "If only I knew what and who He was speaking of and about! He's so confusing, so disturbing!" "Don't be too upset with Him, Thomas and Philip! after all, He chose to reveal Himself to us and not to the world!" Judas exclaimed, "We're going to drive out the Romans and He will rule Judea and all of its territories. I know He will! You'll see, we haven't stuck by Him all these years simply to have Him not take His birth-right. When the time comes for Him to rule, we want to be right there to help Him drive out the Romans and restore all of us to our own birth-rights!" said Judas Iscariot. (cf. John 14:5-21).

"I never expected He would insult our mother as He did!" said John to James. The Zebedee brothers were simply "seizing the opportunity" their very out-spoken and rather vain mother had raised them to expect! They "needed" to be among the rulers in the soon-to-be new kingdom of Jesus Christ. They had, after all, witnessed Him raise Lazarus of Bethany, His closest friend, back to life! Bethany had been such a wonderful place and Lazarus, with Martha and Mary, his sisters were excellent host and hostesses! If He could raise Lazarus from death – and let's not forget all the other miracles He performed on people He didn't even know – then surely He will not forget His apostles!

These men had been with Him from the very beginning! They had, so they believed, every right to the very best He had to offer. Yes, it was wonderful to rest in the beautiful home of Lazarus, but that was not their normal daily fare! Like the Master, they spent most of their time "on the road." They were tired, dirty, sun burned and smelly! That's what "life on the road" did to and for the people of His day. They were doing this because each of the Twelve thought he knew the Master best and that he, as well, knew what was best for the Master! In the end, none of them, save the youngest apostle, John, knew Him at all!! A close examination of their lives and conduct proved that they were a bunch of egotistic, arrogant, selfish and rude men who lacked empathy and ethics and who would deny, doubt and betray the Master in His greatest hour of need!

Sometimes, as the saying goes, we're so close to the forest that we can't see the trees! They were so close to Christ, they didn't see who He really was! They hadn't much faith in Him but they did have great expectations of Him!

Submission to God's will would take them a lifetime to accomplish. First, they would have to stop long enough to hear what He was saying. That, in itself, would take a miracle! Filled with themselves, they had no room for the real

Jesus. If they had telephones in those days one might joke: they didn't take His incoming calls! Secondly, they would need to ponder the messages He spoke to the multitudes. They would need to ask Him "thought-filled" questions about these teachings. Thirdly, if they really got to know Him and simply had not "spent the time of day" with Him, they might learn to really like Him, maybe even grow to love Him! They wouldn't give Him a chance.

We cannot love what we do not know. We cannot know what we do not understand and we cannot understand unless we listen, ponder, and hear. All of these men, in so far as we know, with the exception of John, never got to truly know Jesus Christ! How could they love Him whom they did not even truly know?

To spend time with someone is not necessarily the way to get to know that person. We need to spend a special kind of time, quality time! What is quality time? It seems to me, following the advice of Our Blessed Lord, that quality time is spent in listening to the other, hearing what the other is really saying as the other really says it and then responding to the other. Since the quality time we spend with Christ is time we spend with God the Creator, we have the serious obligation to listen to His definition of who we are, why He made us and what His plans are for us! We are made for heaven, for spending our life firmly rooted in God both now (here on earth) and hereafter (in heaven).

Since real love (agapè) is, so to speak, "Christ's blood" and since Christ is God, that which makes God, God, is love! 1 John says it clearly: "God is love!" (1 John 4:16b). If we are going to communicate with love (the absolute agapè), we must learn to become Divine lovers! We simply cannot call ourselves God-lovers and live our lives rooted and grounded, and slaves to ways of life that are not fully rooted and grounded in the total, entire and complete teachings of Jesus Christ! We are not to be "grocery store" Christians who pick and choose those items from the shelves of Christ's total Gospel we think we need and when we need them! When we permit God to be God, we surrender to His ways! We spend time alone with the Lord and the Gospel, His Divine Word! We spend time with opened minds and opened hearts so that the Holy Spirit might fill us, in ways known only to God, with the many qualities of Divine love needed to communicate on an honest level with God.

Love, Divine love, is never easy! The Church teaches us the authentic meaning of Christ's Gospel. It explains the Gospel for us and, through its teaching authority, it interprets the Gospel for us. In the *Catechism of the Catholic Church*, (cf. Urlic et Orlic Communications, St. Martin de Porres Community, 3050 Gap Road, New Hope, Kentucky 40052. Tel. 502-325-3061. Fax. 502-325-3091), and its *Companion*, (a compendium of Texts referred to in the *Catechism of the Catholic Church*), we have two essential volumes every serious minded Catholic should own, read, ponder and pray! Yes, pray the *Catechism!* If we ponder, we will eventually wind up praying the *Catechism!* We will think about the revealed truth therein contained and we will find these texts to complete the picture of the authentic revealed Jesus Christ, Second Person of the Most Blessed Trinity, Son of God, Son of Mary, one of us yet the same as the Creator, our true and only God, our way to the Father's home and our destiny. Amen!

CONTEMPLATION – PRAYER

Lord, on the Mountain of Transfiguration Your Divinity was bursting through the cloak of Your human nature. In the presence of Moses and Elijah from beyond the grave, and Peter, James and John, our fellow pilgrims, You were strengthened to make the trip to Jerusalem where You were delivered into the hands of sinful men and suffered and died for all of us and for each of us. We want to get to know You better. We want to feel Your pain as You experienced our pain! You became man so that God could know the meaning of a felt, learned experience, the vulnerable experience of living and dying.

Lord, all too often we have asked You and asked You and asked You again to give us everything we need and many things we don't need. It seems we only remember Your Presence when we do have felt needs! We expect You to answer, to respond to these needs immediately. Even when we make novenas or pray rosaries, they are usually encumbered with some "felt need" we "must bring before You"! We never (or seldom) spend time just pondering (really letting Your thoughts fill our minds). We never gaze at a sun rise or sunset and stand in awe at how You could have made anything so beautiful! Then You gave to us men and women, boys and girls, the ability to think, to create, to make our lives so very easy. If only we acted accordingly.

Lord, we are made up of body, which puts us in touch with the physical world; mind which puts us in touch with the rational world; spirit, which has the ability to put us in touch with Your heaven, Your world! We seldom, if ever, have difficulty seeing and experiencing the fruits of our body's labors or the labors of our minds. We are rewarded by comfortable living conditions in quality surroundings when we put our bodies and our minds to work. Interestingly enough, that one part of us that seems to suffer and never learn is our spirit! Yet, it is our spirit that contains the real us!

Lord, we speak today of "our religion" or "his/her religion" as if our relationship with You is simply reduced to a piece of property, an insurance policy. Can You ever imagine a newly and happily married couple describing their love as simply "something I own or put on a shelf?" Yet, that is exactly how we treat You! We don't speak of our oneness with You as a relationship! We should! But ... we don't!

Help me, Lord, to see You in the many stages of Your growth from the moment of Your mother's "Yes" to great Gabriel, to that moment You ascended into heaven! Help me to retrace again and again the great and small events of Your life, Your mother's life, the life of Your step-father, Joseph. Help me in this journey to stand back from each gospel cameo and scene, help me to picture it, and to find You and Your loved ones in it and then spend time listening to You and them, to Your conversations with theirs.

Lord, let me not watch the clock or be distracted with the many burdens I bring with me to prayer. Let me experience Your miracle of love. Let me live in this world ready to slip into Your eternity whenever You summon me. Help me to work at my salvation as if I would live forever; help me to live as if I would die in You, my love, my best friend, my God and my eternal home, now and forever!

Amen!

HIS WILL IN MY LIFE

I will really attempt to give Jesus quality time each and every day. I will not rush my communication with Him. I will spend time where He is in the various Gospel scenes. I will try to picture the scene; see Him and the other people with whom He speaks and be among their number. I will listen to Him and hear Him as He reviews my life and helps me discern how to make good decisions about my life, my relationships, my values and my destiny.

I will try to close-out this holy time with a faith-filled resolution based on the topic of my meditation. When I retire for the evening I will make this examination of conscience the topic of a sacramental encounter with Jesus in the sacrament of reconciliation (Penance).

I will dwell on how I look to God knowing I am as I see myself (usually untrue objectively), as others see me (usually untrue as well) and as God sees me, how I really am! I will remember that to live is to change and to be perfect is to have changed often! Change based on becoming more Christ-like, more close to Him who is my closest Friend here and forever. Amen!

CHAPTER FIVE

How did Jesus pray?
What can I learn about how
to pray from the life of Jesus Christ?
How can this help me to get through
life?

The gospels of Matthew and Luke contain the wonderful prayer we call the Lord's prayer or the "Our Father." I prefer Matthew to Luke as I think it gives a clearer commentary.

Matthew

"Pray then like this:
Our Father who art in heaven,
Hallowed be Thy name.
Thy kingdom come,
Thy will be done,
on earth as it is in heaven.
Give us this day our daily bread;
And forgive us our debts,
As we also have forgiven our debtors;
And lead us not into temptation,
But deliver us from evil."
(Matt. 6:9-13)

Luke

"And he said to them,
'When you pray say:
Father, hallowed be
Thy name.
Thy kingdom come.

Give us each day
our daily bread;
and forgive us our sins,
for we ourselves forgive
everyone who is indebted
to us; and lead us not
into temptation'."
(Luke 12:2-4)

Jesus, in Matthew, comments: "For if you forgive men their trespasses, your heavenly Father also will forgive you; but if you do not forgive men their trespasses, neither will your Father forgive your trespasses." (Matt 6:14-15).

So many books have been written on the Lord's Prayer. I remember, as a student in Austin, Texas, many years ago, a wise priest saying that if you put all of the books together, it (the line of books) would reach across the country! Be that true or not, the "Our Father" is the prayer common to all Christian people and everyone with whom one speaks has an opinion on the meaning of the prayer!

Jesus prayed and made His will known to Almighty God. He adored the Father, He petitioned the Father for the many needs of mankind, He certainly made reparation for sins and He offered thanks to the Father for the loving care given by the Father. He often sought His Father's presence in lonely places, all alone! He needed time to be with His Father! In the great priestly prayer of Jesus and from the prayer, we get a great insight into the quality of the Lord's relationship with the Father.

Reprinted here is the high priestly prayer of the Lord as found in John 17. The entire chapter is devoted to it as, I believe, it to be the very soul of the Lord's prayer.

Completion of Jesus Work

After he had spoken these
words, Jesus looked up to
heaven and said:

"Father, the hour has come!
Give glory to Your Son
that Your Son may give glory to
You,

inasmuch as You have given Him
authority over all mankind,
that He may bestow eternal life
on those You gave Him.

Eternal life is this:
to know You, the only true God,
and Him Whom You have sent,
Jesus Christ.

I have given You glory on earth
by finishing the work You gave
Me to do.

Do You now, Father, give Me
glory at Your side,
a glory I had with You before
the world began.

I have made Your name known
to those You gave Me out of the
world.
These men You gave Me were
Yours;
they have kept Your word.

Now they realize
that all that You gave Me comes
from You.

I entrusted to them
the message You entrusted to Me,
and they received it.

They have known that in truth I
came from You,
they have believed it was You
who sent Me."

Prayer for the Disciples

"For these I pray –
not for the world
but for these You have given Me,
for they are really Yours.

Just as all that belongs to Me
is Yours,
so all that belongs to You is
Mine.
It is in them that I have been
glorified.

I am in the world no more,
but these are in the world
as I come to You.
O Father most holy,
protect them with Your Name
which You have given Me.
that they may be one, even as
We are one.

As long as I was with them,
I guarded them with Your Name
which You gave Me.
I kept careful watch,
and not one of them was lost,

none but him who was destined
to be lost –
in fulfillment of Scripture.

Now, however, I come to You;
I say all this while I am still in
the world
that they may share My joy
completely.

I gave them Your word,
and the world has hated them
for it;
they do not belong to the world
any more than I belong to the
world.

I do not ask You to take them
out of the world,
but to guard them from the evil
one.

They are not of the world,
any more than I belong to the
world.

Consecrate them by means of
truth –
'Your word is truth.'

As You have sent Me into the
world,
so I have sent them into the world;

*I consecrate Myself for their
sakes now,
that they may be consecrated in truth."*

Prayer for All Believers

*"I do not pray for them alone.
I pray also for those who will
believe in Me through their
word,*

*that all may be one
as You, Father, are in Me, and I
in You;
I pray that they may be one in
Us,
that the world may believe that
You sent Me.*

*I have given them the glory You
gave Me
that they may be one, as We are
one –*

*I living in them, You living Me –
that their unity may be complete.
So shall the world know that
You sent Me.
and that You loved them as You
loved Me.*

*Father,
all those You gave Me*

I would have in My company
where I am,
to see this glory of Mine
which is Your gift to Me,
because of the love You bore Me
before the world began.

Just Father,
the world has not known You,
but I have known You;
and these men have known that
You sent Me.

To them I have revealed Your
Name,
and I will continue to reveal It
so that Your love for Me may
live in them,
and I may live in them."

In the first section of the prayer, the Lord Jesus beautifully expresses His understanding of the mission He has received from the Father, that is, to give glory to the Father by exercising the authority of the Messiah over all mankind. The authority and its exercise is given in order to bring humanity to eternal life. Eternal life is defined as the intimate knowledge (living experience of) the Godhead and His Son, Jesus Christ. The Lord tells of His oneness with the Father, a oneness that existed prior to creation! The Lord tells that He indeed made known the Father's name (Abba) (familiar for "Dad") to the disciples. He "grades" the performance of the disciples by saying that they have kept the Messiah's wish by keeping the Father's word. He speaks of entrusting the disciples with the Father's message! The disciples will teach the Message!

In the second section, the Lord prays for the disciples. He refuses to pray for the (evil) world and places His focus on the "redeeming" world, He prays for this world. He ties the disciples into Himself and speaks of all of them going to the Father. He prays that the Father will protect the disciples and guard them as He (the Son) guarded them. He asks the Father to consecrate them by means of truth. The truth to which He refers is the truth of Messianic revelation. His message is profound: the disciples are to carry the word of God; the disciples are to be extensions of the Father and the Son and the Spirit and the Blessed Trinity is to live within the disciple! The disciple is destined to go to heaven. There the Lord will be to welcome His disciples provided they continue to make known here on earth the Trinity while they are living on earth.

It is important to note the method and structure of this high priestly prayer. Throughout the prayer, Jesus reviews again and again His relationship with His Father and He speaks of the job He is here on earth to do!

He is as clear as one can be in His explanation about who the disciple is (his identity) and the specific relationship of the disciple and the Master! The Blessed Trinity has a relationship with the disciple by means of the Messiah!

The prayer is fully human. It is familial. It is warm and comforting while at the same time being deeply challenging. Jesus Christ knows exactly Who He is, Who the Father is and who the disciple is. He knows what the mission is and He knows how the disciple is to fulfill the mission!

One could not read this Chapter without seeing the tremendous love (agapè) of the members of the Trinity for one another. One could not read John's chapter without knowing the role and place in the life of the Father and the Son the disciple has! On earth, the disciple is the "tabernacle" of the Trinity!

This is the essence of prayer and worship. In prayer, as has been repeatedly said, we make our wills known to God. In worship we integrate God's will into our lives. The great high priestly prayer is totally colored by emotion and devotion. Jesus "feels" every word of the prayer. He is in every word. He owns it; He personifies it; He gives it His flesh and blood. Jesus' devotion is felt. It is the bridge between His prayer and the worship He performs. In worship He fully does God's will! In worship, He is the victim. In prayer, He is the priest! He is priest and victim! He speaks on our behalf and He offers Himself to the Father in sacrifice for our sins. He is the embodiment of the "Our Father." He has seen the will of God come to the earth and He had made intercession for His followers. He has forgiven the sins of the sinful and has made Himself the Lamb of sacrifice. Truly, as the old saying goes: Lovers see themselves through rose-colored glasses. When God looks on us, He sees us through the blood of His Son.

Amen!

THE UNSPOKEN – THE HIDDEN

Lord, Jesus Christ, for centuries, men have tried to discover how much knowledge You had of the Blessed Trinity before You were born, when Your Mother Mary carried You in her womb. Did You know the profound mysteries of God as You lay in Bethlehem's manger? Did You comprehend what You would accomplish as our Messiah and Lord when You were learning how, as a baby, to walk? When You were a teenager, teaching the priests of the Old Testament in the Temple, did You already know the hidden meaning behind the great truths of Jewish revelation?

As a baby, young adolescent, and man, You learned by experience what all of us learn and experience. You were "cut no slack" and You cut yourself no slack! You had to experience the terrible pain of seeing the people of Your village, Your time and country, deliberately turn their backs on You! Speak to us, Lord Jesus!

"They thought I couldn't understand what the heavenly choirs sang over the hills of Bethlehem that cold December night. I was too young, a newborn infant. How could an infant understand? These poor people. They still thought they could figure out how and why God became man! They applied all the rules of their logic, all the truths of discovery to that which was totally illogical, that is, the unconditional love of the Creator for His creatures; a love that is God's essence – God is love! No creature is ever given the answer to how much I knew as an Infant or how much I knew as a young Man! It is recorded in Scripture that as a 12-year-old Boy, I taught the teachers when I spent those days in the Temple! I was 12-years-old! I had no time to waste. I had to be about my Father's work, so don't try to figure out what I knew, how I knew it or when I knew it!

I told you that no one knows the Father but the Son and no one knows the Son but the Father, and anyone who wishes to see the Father must be invited to do so by the Son! I told you that before Creation, the Father and I were one! Before the world began, the Father and I were in glory! Still, with human minds you seek to fathom the unfathomable! The finite can never understand the infinite! Just as you cannot put the ocean's full contents into a glass, so you cannot put God (the infinite) into your (finite) minds without the means I gave you, the Holy Eucharist! The Church!

At the Last Supper, I took bread and changed it into My Body; I took the cup of wine and turned it into My Blood. I then told you to continue to do this down through the ages, to make Me present among you! The way to understand the Creator is to follow the words I gave you and imitate the lifestyle I lived. Yes, we cannot all live walking from town to town, village to village, preaching, teaching and being a miracle worker. We are all different; we are all unique. We must all let God be God and take care of our own destiny and that "destiny" is why I came here in the first place! You must try to think as I think, try to understand the world as I understood the world. The overall priority in your lives must be My Father's will! You must give His will the foremost place in your life.

You want to follow Me because where I go you want to go! If you try with all your strength to follow Me, where I go you shall go! You must sincerely and faithfully try to go where I am. I am the way to heaven; I have told you the truth about heaven; I am the life you will live in heaven! The language of heaven is the love I live and I taught you to live! You must live on in My love. This means you must practice

My love! You must take care when you are humiliated to set aside all resentment. You must never be disturbed and allow yourself to become angry and hostile toward others. You must try to remain kindly and friendly, filled with loving thoughts and no hidden resentment! You must hope in My Father's ways. In the end, that will see you safely into heaven. Believe in Me!

Attitude plays a very important part in winning your salvation. Try to have a positive attitude about life. You are in the world but you are not of the world. You belong to Me and to My Father. The reason I sent the Holy Spirit, the Spirit of My Father and Me, is to help you to understand the most important things in life. Remember, you can take nothing but your good deeds with you when you die. Nothing else can ever go with you! As the old saying goes, the shroud has no pockets!

There are so very many people today who spend their whole lives saying they love God but living otherwise! What I mean is this: they save and hoard money and the material goods of this world. They never bother to give out of their "plenty" let alone out of their need! They are totally unready to enter heaven. They forget that as you live so shall you die. They don't realize the message of the talents, the moral or lesson behind the corporal works of mercy! They think the Beatitudes were spoken only to individuals and not to the wealthy nations of the world! Unready, ill prepared and selfish, they expect to live forever. They do not see the Father's will; they think they have eternal life right now! They resent My faithful disciples because the lives of My faithful disciples convict them of their sinfulness and they hate the true disciples because of this.

Strive to enter My Father's home by the narrow gate. This "gate" is the opening to heaven. Follow Me, imitate My example. Put the Father's ways first and all else will follow. Seek ye first the kingdom of God and justice – all else will take care of itself.

I will see you! You will see Me! Together, in the company of My Mother and all of heaven, you and I will experience God forever! Always remember and never forget: the finite can never hold the Infinite but the Infinite can hold the whole of the finite! You will never understand God, but He will always understand you and never leave you – even now you live in the hollow of His hand!

I go to the home I have prepared for you, I told My disciples; I told My heavenly Father that We, the Father and I, will live in the hearts of Our true disciples. I prayed for you when I asked the Father to protect all those who, through the words of the first disciples, heard My words and acted accordingly.

You are Mine, live and love as I have taught you to do so that we can be together in our Father's home forever!"

Amen!

CONTEMPLATION – PRAYER

Father, You gave Jesus Christ, Your Son, the Son of Mary, the glory He always had with You, the glory of the Blessed Trinity, Father, Son and Holy Spirit. You have enabled Him to find a way to always remain with us. In the Word, the holy Scriptures, we have the guide to our salvation. In the sacraments, we have the touchstones of and to Divinity and the eternal Presence of Jesus Christ. These sacraments enable us to touch Him and in touching Him to touch You. Through them, You touch us and our lives! Especially, in the first Easter sacrament, Penance or Reconciliation, You give us Your forgiveness for those sins of commission and many acts of omission of good which we failed to do.

You have prayed for us, Lord Jesus. You taught us to pray and You gave us the grace to truly love You. Grace, Your Divine help, never hinders or impedes our free will. Because You, O God, made us for Yourself, You desire us to do all in our power to incarnate, to incorporate, Your will in our lives.

Lord, when You prayed to Your Father, what did You see? What must He be like? You told Philip, Your disciple, that he who sees You sees the Father, that You and the Father are one and the same! Lord Jesus, show me the face of the Father. Let me see Your face and I will see God! Lord Jesus, often I don't know how to pray, what to say! Lord, the cares and concerns of so many in the world which come to me through the media, the television, radio and newspapers, weigh me down! The temptations of the world, my own flesh and the devil, discourage me; yet, O Lord, through them all, I stay focused on You, my Redeemer, my best Friend and Brother. You, Lord, in the end, You are all I have!

Jesus, You gave me Your mother from the cross. You asked her to receive me as her son (daughter). You asked me to understand that my true home, Your home, is heaven! You gave me Your Father's intimate name, not Lord, but "Abba," Daddy! You responded to Your mother and Your Father as a son, as a child! You taught me that unless I become as a little child, I shall not enter the kingdom of heaven. Please, Lord, take me and make me childlike! Give me the wisdom of the ages and the innocence of newborn babes. Help me to see beyond the complexities of life to the simplicity of the true, the good and the beautiful of Your creation, of Your life, of Your witness.

Father, I will to live with You in eternity. Help me to prepare for eternity here and now by living in Jesus and Mary. As Mary found her true identity in her Son, so help me to appreciate Mary the first disciple of Jesus! When she gave her "Yes" to the great Archangel Gabriel, she became not only the Mother of God; she became the first disciple of the newly "incarnated" Messiah! Mary's every wish, her every desire was rooted and grounded in God's will. Her expressions of love flowered in God's will being celebrated here on earth and in her will. She became totally submerged in the Father's will and, as such, became for all of us the bridge leading to Jesus, God Incarnate.

Mary looked into her Son's eyes and saw the Godhead. Jesus looked into Mary's eyes and saw the dream His Father had when He created mankind. In Mary, God loved His own perfect reflection. In Mary, Jesus experienced creation before the fall of mankind. In Mary, God gave all of us a way to approach Himself. Mary's "yes" to God gave us Jesus. Mary's "yes" to our needs gives us to Jesus. She is the perfect reflection in creation of what God shares with us and she is for us the best we can share with God! Mary is the ideal of created love and the soul-model each of us struggles to imitate. She is immaculate, without any stain of sin, original sin or actual sin. She is totally one with the Creator in His Divine plan for all of us.

Like any good Mother, Mary treats each of us and all of us as if we were her only children, her only child! She mirrors what God wants of us in His own dreams for all of us and each of us! She is God's dream for mankind. She was and is perfect. She has chosen to spend her eternity – or a goodly part of it – making intercession on our behalf before God's throne!

When Jesus prays to His Father, I have no doubt that it was His mother who taught Him how first to pray! I have no doubt that it was Mary who told Him the first things He learned – from a human perspective, a created or creative perspective – about the Father! It was Mary and Joseph who explained why He had to pray and what prayer accomplished. The prayer of the Son is that of the Mother. The prayer of the Mother is always that of the Son.

Created images of the Father come from our lived experiences. In Our Lady and in Our Lord we have the perfect approach to prayer and worship. As they lived the Father's will, so they ask us to try to live like them. As they celebrate eternity in God's home, so they invite us to live in them as they live in the Godhead (heaven). God is all-in-all to Jesus and Mary. The true disciples are all-in-all to the Holy Family of Nazareth and are brought before the Blessed Trinity by the patron of a happy death, St. Joseph; they are given to the Son by the Mother and they are placed in the Father's love through the human nature of the Son. This is heaven: to experience God living in the humanity of Jesus (His sacred heart) which is held in the always immaculate heart of Mary, and ever guarded by St. Joseph. Amen!

HIS WILL IN MY LIFE

I promise to pray as Jesus taught me. I promise to reflect on the great high priestly prayer of Jesus as found in the gospel of John, chapter 17. I will try to read and ponder this chapter at least once a week and try to understand what the Lord is saying to His Father and apply it to my life.

I will strive to work each day as if I would live forever and live as if I would die today. I promise to spend at least a few minutes each day alone with the Holy Family of Jesus, Mary and Joseph and imagine how they pray to the Father. I will remind myself that I must pray like them if I am to truly appreciate the home I will call heaven.

Finally, I will strive to rid myself of sin by living a disciplined life and by making frequent use of the sacraments and by praying the rosary, Gabriel's song, the Church's prayer and my final wish as, at the hour of my death, I hear Jesus say, "I have heard my mother speak of you."

I will remind myself each day that I have all eternity to rest and that that the quality of my eternal rest will be determined by the quality of my work for God here and now!

Amen!

CHAPTER SIX

WHAT WERE THE GREAT THEMES (THOUGHTS) OF JESUS CHRIST? HOW DO I PUT THEM INTO MY OWN INTERIOR LIFE?

In the desert, at the beginning of His public ministry, Jesus encountered Satan. The devil tempted Him to break His special vows of retreat. He responded to each of the temptations: "Not on bread alone shall man live (but on every word that comes from the mouth of God)." (Luke 4:4); "You (the devil) shall do homage to the Lord your God; Him alone shall you adore." (Luke 4:8). "(Luke 4:12).

Each of His responses to the Evil One put the devil in his place! It showed the superiority of Jesus Christ and it demonstrated how each of us should meet evil and send the "devil packing"! To resist temptation is the first of the major themes of the Lord's life! Clearly, the devil would do anything to destroy Jesus and His gospel. Where Jesus or His disciples are, you can be sure to see an outpouring of the evil one! The fact that we have temptations proves we may very well be worth winning as a prize! Certainly, Satan sees it that way!

The combat between good and evil is always present in our lives! We see how Jesus resisted temptation and we are called to do likewise. Note that He was tempted while on retreat; He was tempted when He was doing something good (preparing to do God's will); He was tempted when He was weak from fasting during a long desert retreat of prayer and, no doubt, of planning His ministry.

Certainly, a major theme of His ministry is resistance to all inroads of evil in our lives.

A second major theme is that of clarification of the meaning of the various prophecies concerning the Messiah. He does this repeatedly, most especially He does this in preaching and in performing miracles as demonstrations of His preaching's authority. It is certainly interesting to note that as time goes on in His public ministry, and as He performs more and more public miracles, He cautions those recipients of the miracle not to tell anyone about the cure or gift of health or new life. He cautions them to show themselves to the Jewish priest and to offer thanks to Almighty God for the favor received. He seems to be uncomfortable with the fact that crowds came to Him because of the miracles. He really wanted them to listen to His teaching, to weigh His words in the light of their own conduct and to form a moral decision to change their lives for the better was the focus of all His teachings. His followers would be given great graces if only they would listen and hear what the Master taught. The problem with the miracles was that everyone wanted one but few wanted to live the morality the Lord taught!

Like John the Baptist who grew terribly angry with the crowds who saw the simple water baptism as "all they had to do" to have their sins forgiven, Jesus too resented people hanging on Him solely to get a "quick cure." For this reason, He stressed the essence of conversion: to love by going the distance in self-denial in order to incarnate God's will in my flesh! To live and to love as Jesus lived and loved is the key to discipleship!

Still another theme is that of proclaiming (living, speaking) the reign of God. Luke 9 is the text which speaks of this. What is the reign of God? Simply, to allow God's kingdom to come on earth as that kingdom is lived in heaven. The reign of God is heaven literally lived and celebrated here on earth. Jesus calls us to pray – in His name – together! He calls us to live and love one another as He lives and loves in us. He wants us to feed the hungry not only the physically starving, but the spiritually starved as well. There are many ways in which a person is hungry, thirsty, naked, imprisoned, homeless, etc. We see those unfortunates everywhere we look. Some of the greatest "poverty" I know is in the mansions of the wealthy!

For over two years – in recent years – I visited my dear mother in a nursing home. I saw scores of elderly without even one visitor. One old lady said to me: "Father, I won't have anyone to cry for me when I die. All my loved ones are gone (dead) and all that are left are strangers." That very next visit – a month later – as I walked into the convalescent home to see my own dear mother who, incidentally died in my arms two months later, the nurses asked me to go directly to the elderly lady's room. She lay very close to death. I always brought the holy oils of anointing with me. I anointed her, gave her absolution and the Apostolic Pardon (the Pope's Blessing at the hour of death). When she took a deep breath and exhaled, I knew she was gone. I was unaware that tears were freely flowing down my face. She did indeed have some of us who cried for her! When the two nurses and the three nurses' aides saw me crying, they cried as well. How good God is! The woman was a great gift to all of us!

Jesus warns us that there is a serious price we will have to pay as His disciples: We will be persecuted because, like Jesus, if we really are like Him, we will anger the arrogant worldly types in our midst! These types are everywhere! They are in power, in the various organizations, in churches, in schools, industry, health care, etc., etc. They look like us, even act like us, but they are fundamentally different from us. Jesus wants us to be sensitive to others. He wants us to be merciful and kind; yet, He wants us to challenge ourselves and others with the pure gospel message! Not having been made for this world, we are destined to spend only a short time here and all eternity living in God through the risen glorified body of Our Lord Jesus Christ.

Clearly, God gave us free will! We can choose to opt for God, His only begotten Son, the Son's revelation or we can choose another way. The simple truth is that the original sin of our first parents, Adam and Eve, blocked our ability to save ourselves. We needed a Messiah, we needed a Redeemer! I hardly think that Almighty God would have put Himself through the events of Calvary just for the sake of demonstrating that He loved us! Calvary was necessary for the Divine justice to be appeased and for the heavenly gates to open wide so you and I could be saved!

I believe we are much "too simplistic" today! We live in a culture, especially in the first world, where we no longer examine our consciences. We no longer really believe we can hurt the Lord by our sins! But what did the events that happened to Saul on the road to Damascus mean if not that the Lord can be hurt, even now! Saul of Tarsus was a real persecutor! He persecuted the Church! The ninth chapter of Acts shouts to us that Jesus in glory, still feels the pain of His disciples! He is still present with us and to us!

"As he (Saul) traveled along and was approaching Damascus, a light from the sky suddenly flashed about him. He fell to the ground and at the same time (he) heard a voice saying, 'Saul, Saul, why do you persecute Me?' 'Who are you, sir?' Saul asked. The voice answered, 'I am Jesus, the One you are persecuting ... .' " (Acts 10:3-5a).

Jesus told us that when we hurt the least of His apostles and disciples, we hurt Him! He promised the faithful disciples that as people treated Him (the Christ) so will they also be treated! God knows how often we feel ourselves to be abused because we believe strongly in our values. It really costs a great deal to live our values! If there is one great theme that Christ teaches, it is that we must see to it that our values reflect His values. Keep in mind that simply "mouthing" values isn't having values! We must live our Christ-centered values.

Today, we live in situation-ethics ethos! If I can find some lame reason to explain aberrant behavior, I can integrate it, calling it "acceptable" and, therefore, I can excuse it! It then becomes part of culture! Look how easy it is to excuse abortion; from the moment of conception to the actual moment of birth (i.e., when the culture decides to confer the rights of "personhood" upon the birthing child) the fetus can be destroyed! Or, for example, how easy it is to explain justice issues away! It is most acceptable for all of us in the first world to ignore the absolute poverty in the third world! By what right can we call this acceptable? By what standard of morality?

One of the things we Catholics fail to do today is to examine our consciences. Using the "modernism philosophy" of excusing, we simply ignore self-examination because we do not want to deal with the consequences of guilt. We do not want to feel guilty. As a result, we can continue to "desensitize" ourselves to each other and to God's laws and to the magisterium (teaching authority) of the Church! Having accomplished this, we set ourselves on the path of the three angels of evil: pleasure, the ultimate good; self-love (egotism); self direction (denial of another authority, a legitimate authority).

Jesus insists on submission to God's holy will. He insists on fidelity in discipleship and He insists that the disciples work hard at winning their own salvation. He has no room in His agenda for idle chatter or senseless talk. He insists that we incarnate the "motto" of Paul: Do the work of an evangelist. Only then will we truly understand the meaning of the word "evangelist," that is, to live, work and even to die like Our Lord Jesus Christ to Whom we glory and honor today, tomorrow and always!

Amen!

THE UNSPOKEN – THE HIDDEN

"I have told you so very often and in so very many ways to resist Satan! I have warned you over and over again that evil is everywhere and seeks to destroy the graces of My Presence and that of My Father and Our Spirit living within you. One of the central themes of My ministry has been to alert you to the presence of the arch-enemy who goes about the world looking for souls to devour! People never think they run the risk of compromising their salvation. People feel they are always justified in the decisions they make. Young people (and many not so young) choose to compromise their own salvation and their neighbors' salvation by violating My Father's commandments, the values I taught you and the ways of life given to My Church to teach and to enforce!

Living together outside of wedded marriage is not permitted; stealing by any means is wrong; failure to relieve the hunger and pain of your sisters and brothers is sinful – most especially if you have the means to do this! Paul, My faithful apostle, but disciple first, correctly taught that all My disciples should struggle and strive to have within themselves the same "mind" (philosophy, theology, lifestyle) as I have! They should think like Me, the truth and the very life of the Father!

Many people today forget that they are made in the image and likeness of God and not the other way around! People today want God to accept evil and call it good! My Father loves the sinner but hates the sin! To call evil, good and good, evil is the philosophy of Satan who claimed to be the Creator though, in fact, he was only a creature!

We cannot serve two masters: My Father and Satan!

You must choose one or the other. Remember what I said about "hot" or "cold." When it comes to God and the things of God you must strive to be on fire (hot) with love for My Father and His ways!

In this day and age, there are in popular cultural views no (or very few) "absolutes." To honor our parents is optional today; to respect legitimate authority is certainly "up for grabs"! Do you see how I honored My Father's wishes? I submitted totally to the will of the eternal God. So many people in the first world are "throw aways." So many: the unborn; the very ill who lack financial means; the elderly; the poor; the emotionally and psychologically unstable – all these are compromised by the forces in control of the first world! There are so many hurting people and they are hurting simply because they are old, physically unattractive and/or poor! It is wrong to treat these people as if they have no rights! It is My Father who gave them human rights when they were conceived; they are all worth the price of the blood I shed for them on Calvary and the Holy Spirit of God lives within them! Who then are those who dismiss these people as worthless?! By what right do they dismiss these good souls as worthless? They are worth the love, interest and care of Almighty God! Treat them all accordingly! This is one of the major ethical and moral lessons of My life and one I want My followers to live! Be brave, speak the truth I taught you!

The Messiah's role is to save humanity by offering reparation to God for the sins committed by humanity. Submission to the Father's will is the overall fundamental theme of My earthly ministry. It is what I came to earth to teach you to do. All human life is sacred to my Father: life within the womb, newborn life, and life of the sick, weak and elderly! The quality of life is also important to My Father. Some people have little or no life. Some people have no quality in their lives or of their lives! My disciples are charged with correcting this!

Each person is called by the Father to have and foster an interior life. Today, so very many people speak of "my religion" or "my Church." What people should speak about is their relationship with God, with Me, with the Holy Spirit and with the Church. A relationship with God is really a deep abiding friendship! A relationship is an awareness of the other person in my life. When that person is upset with me, I am upset; when that "other" is happy with me, I am happy. Your relationship with Me should be personal, yet rooted in the Church; it should be based on a deep "feeling" for Me as My relationship with you is also based on a deep feeling that I have for you.

In My Father's view, eternal life for you can begin now if only My followers would allow it. My Father and I want nothing more than to come to you and by means of the Holy Spirit, to make Our home deep within you. The home of My Father and the Holy Spirit (where I live with Them), the Members of the Most Blessed Trinity, is heaven! Heaven is truly within you when you live actively in My love. To live actively in My love is to be submissive to My heavenly Father's will.

Evil is of two types: one type deals with whole areas of choice. This takes place when one chooses to commit a sin, make a choice to do something that is expressly against God's holy will. The other area deals with omission. This takes place when one chooses to avoid doing what one ought to do. For example, I have spoken in parables. One important parable is the parable of the talents. You know what I said about the man who refused to invest his God given talents. He was not doing God's will. Sins of omission and sins of commission are offenses against the very nature of your destiny! You were created to know, love and serve God and to be happy with God forever. You were told by Me how you are to win your salvation. You were given an example that as I did, you too should go and do.

It is the will of My Father that all He has given Me shall never leave Me. I want My own to be within My heart. As I live in my Mother's immaculate heart, so My disciples, living in My sacred heart, will live in My Mother, Spouse of the Eternal God.

My immaculate Mother said "Yes" to the eternal Creator. By means of the Holy Spirit, I was incarnated (became flesh) within the womb of My mother. God the Son becomes a Man so that mankind will have a way back to God. This central theme of My life is the fundamental theme of your life. We are all called to find our permanent home with and in God by means of My life and by the help of the Holy Spirit."

Amen!

CONTEMPLATION – PRAYER

Lord Jesus, I am a bundle of appetites seeking to be satisfied! My body, my mind and my soul seek fulfillment in You. But often, I do not want You. Often, I become tired of You and find physical beauty elsewhere! I know, O Lord, You are within me and You created me for Yourself. I know that my destiny is tied into Your will for me. I know that I belong to You and to not another soul! You have taught me that real Christ-like love is rooted and grounded in supernatural love for my neighbor. That love begins and ends with You, my God. It wills for my neighbor the greatest good that could come to my neighbor, that is desiring and willing the ultimate union of my neighbor's soul with and in God.

Whenever I try to deny the reason why I was made or the reason why my neighbor was made, by being egocentric, selfish and hostile to Your will, I play directly into the hands of Satan. The devil wants me to be discouraged. The devil wants to divert my will from You. O Beauty, ever Ancient and always New! I remember what You said when You taught us of that constant warfare existing between the body, (the material), and the soul, the spiritual!

The devil tries to discourage me by finding reasons and planting them in and along my way in life. Reasons to choose evil over good; reasons why I should play the ancient Job and "curse God and die!" I won't do this, O Lord! I refuse to permit myself to give into myself, to justify evil!

There are so many things that get in the way of my salvation: My physical needs, my intellectual and emotional needs even my supernatural spiritual needs at times create problems for me as I struggle to stay on the straight and narrow pilgrims' path to heaven. When someone compliments me on being a good person or on doing a good job, do I really stop and thank God for permitting this person to catch a glimmer of God's love from my actions, words or deeds? Do I remind myself that unless – in the final analysis – the Lord builds the house, in vain do the builders labor! Unless the Lord keep the watch, in vain do the guards keep vigil!? Clearly, the Lord is "in charge!" Whenever I try to be "in charge" things will get compromised!

Lord, You have taught me that true freedom is submission to the Father's will. This is my "final cause," the reason why I was made. Lord, You have caused me to be dissatisfied with anything and everything which is against Your holy will. As Mary, Your Mother, found her ultimate happiness in doing Your will, so I ask You for that grace to find my own happiness in Your holy will.

A droplet of water mixes with the wine to be offered in the chalice to God; two pieces of wax melt into one; the ocean of God's love takes the tiny streams of my love and submerges them, loses them in the infinite ocean of Divinity. They are now part and parcel of God in His human nature, in Christ Jesus. This is the true meaning of Jesus Christ's thinking.

I must contemplate Your life and Your love, Lord. I must see my doubt in doubting Thomas; my denial in the denial of Peter; my betrayal in the conduct of Judas Iscariot. I must see Your eyes as Peter saw them, when they (the guards) escorted You out of the high priest's courtyard on Holy Thursday; I must feel Your kiss as Judas felt Your lips that fateful night in the Garden. I must learn to be like Magdalene who never gave up, who was far braver on Calvary than when – earlier on – she was compromised as a prostitute! I must learn the docility of Mary and the goodness of Martha, the sisters of Lazarus of Bethany. I must have the patience of the old crippled man sitting by the pool awaiting the stirring of the waters. I must have the faith of the centurian and look to him to give me hope when my faith begins to fail. I must be zealous for You as were James and John Zebedee. Lord, I must search the New Testament to find myself, my true nature and my way to Your arms. Help me to see myself in all of the peoples of Your life and, dear Lord, help me to transform the countless stumbling blocks of my own life into stepping stones leading to where You are now, living forever in the Father's arms.

Amen!

HIS WILL IN MY LIFE

I resolve, dear Lord, to spend time pondering the Scriptures, especially, the New Testament. I will keep a journal as I study the many people of the New Testament and try to situate them into Your friends and Your enemies. Then I will try to see myself and my own place where they are and where I want to be.

Lord, I will pray often and be careful never to disappoint You by not keeping guard over my senses. I will remind myself that the eye is the window of the soul and the thought is parent to the deed! In this way I will guard my senses and make myself ready, a heart beat away from now to be with You.

I promise to pray my rosary daily meditating on the mysteries of the rosary in the hope that Our Lady, Your Mother and mine, will use the rosary to "raise me" as she raised You in the Father's love.

I promise You, Lord, that I will try never to disappoint You by forgetting that You are as near to me as my next breath and as real to me as the next beat of my heart!

Amen!

CHAPTER SEVEN

*WHAT MUST I EXPECT IF I LIVE
(OR TRY TO LIVE)
CLOSE TO JESUS AS ONE OF HIS DISCIPLES?*

"If you find that the world hates you, know it has hated Me before you. If you belonged to the world, it would love you as its own; the reason it hates you is that you do not belong to the world." (John 15:18,19).

Our Lord said these words to His friends, His followers, and His apostles. Are they accurate? Are they real? Will we be hated because we belong to Jesus Christ? Will the world and its forces truly seek to harm us in body, mind and spirit because we are one with the Lord? The answer is, yes! I must expect hatred and persecution if I try to be close to Jesus Christ. To be close to Christ means to be His follower living, thinking, acting, praying as He did and as He taught us to do! It means putting myself "on the line" for Him! In other words, I have no other choice, if I live as His disciple, but to live life as Jesus would have me to do.

In this world there are countless ideologies, philosophies, and cultural modes of life that are in direct and indirect conflict with the teachings of Christ. As Roman Catholics, we believe that Our Divine Lord founded our Church and gave it a teaching authority and gave it the sacraments to sustain us in God's love. I'm sure it comes as no surprise when I state that I know of, and I'm sure you know of, people within the Church who hold totally different views and continue to govern some of our organizations and other agencies. This is simply the way it is. Often, there is conflict within the Church because of differing ecclesiologies (views of Church), the role of authority within the Church, how the organizations of the various Church institutions interact with one another, etc. All of this, at times, creates tension and makes for high emotional expressions!

When I studied the philosophies of literature, I learned that where there are multiple personalities, there are "conflict breathing/breeding zones"! The whole antagonist vs.

protagonist theme is predicated on conflict. Whenever we have differing issues we have grounds which are, at times, more like battlefields than campgrounds!

Conflict, hatred, uncomfortable "life situations," rejection, alienation, sometimes isolation, persecution and sacrifice are all part and parcel of what we can expect as disciples of Jesus Christ. So much for the negative! Now for the positive:

"Do not let your hearts be troubled,
Have faith in God and faith in Me.
In My Father's house there are
many dwelling places; otherwise,
how could I have told you that I was
going to prepare a place for you?
I am indeed going to prepare a place for you,
and then I shall come back to take you with Me
that where I am you also may be. ..." (John 14:1-3).

"You know me, you have been with Me day and night since I called you to be My disciples. I have told you that heaven for you and for Me will be the same. Together, We will experience the infinite all-loving good God. Since you are a part of My mystical body, you will experience the Blessed Trinity through My human nature, My human, risen, glorified body and soul! Don't you understand? Don't you comprehend? The finite (you) will experience the infinite (God) living in, with and through Me; yet, you will still be yourself with your unique personality, history, emotional life and, at the resurrection on the last day, with a new glorified body as well. You will be able to experience the whole event of creation! You will be totally within the essence of My happiness and love. You will see God! Remember what I told Dismas, the good thief: "Today, you will be with Me in paradise!" Remember why My apostles were called: to make Me known throughout Jerusalem and to all corners of the world. With Thomas, My doubting apostle who confessed – after he had seen me: 'My Lord and My God' – I said: 'Because you have seen Me, Thomas, you believe, blessed are those who have not seen and who believe.'

I fully know that I exact a great price from you who do not physically see Me with your eyes. Yet, I want you to know that My grace will always be sufficient for you to achieve the heights of heaven. You must follow Me in the same way that I followed My Father's will. Nailed to a cross, unable to move, I led people of all times and places into heaven. Like a grain of seed that must die for the flower to bloom, so you must die to yourself to your egotism and pride in order that I might grow within you. You think you have questions about these things; think of the countless questions My mother and My stepfather had about those many events surrounding My birth, early life and even My public life! Look at the little people from whom most people ran: look at little Zachaeus whom I called down from the sycamore tree in order to stay in his home (Luke 19:1-10). Here was a truly good man but misunderstood by all because he really wasn't what they thought him to be. Look at the woman caught in adultery (cf. John 8:1-12) and whom everyone wanted to stone. My own mother was under suspicion and suspected of being in that position at one time and she could have been stoned! Look at the poor widow who gave all she had to God (cf. Luke 21:1-4). The events of My earthly life are packed with people who could have asked: why me? But they did not ask. They were truly humble and found goodness and this led them to find God.

Jerusalem is the type of the eternal City of Peace, My home in heaven. I cried over the earthly City of Jerusalem because they did not recognize the path to the eternal peace which God had made known throughout the ages. (Luke 19:41-44). As a result of that rejection, the earthly City was destroyed. I tried and I tried to get them to see who I am. I explained to them their own Scriptures, I said to them: 'How can they say that the Messiah is the son of David? Does not David himself say in the psalms, (The Lord said to my lord: sit at my right hand while I make your enemies your footstool)? Now, if David accords him the title, Lord, how can the Messiah be David's son?' They couldn't answer because they were filled with their own pride!

I have often thought, how foolish so many people are! They see beautiful created things and they are so very impressed. They loved the beauty of the Temple adorned with precious stones and votive offerings. I told them the day would come when not one stone will be left on another, but it will all be torn down. (cf. Luke: 21:5-6).

Even today, you see so many signs and wonders and you do not seem to understand. There are signs in the sun, the moon, the stars; nations are in greater anguish today because of selfishness than at any other time; natural events are taking place that truly frighten you as you see the powers of heaven and earth shaken. Still, you keep placing trust in the created, the artificial and the human. (cf. Luke 21:25-28). When will you learn?

Try to focus on that which is truly eternal. Try to place all your trust in Me and in the values I taught you by My life and My death. Then, a heartbeat from now, you shall see God and, living within Me through the grace of the Holy Spirit, We shall experience heaven forever."

Amen!

THE UNSPOKEN – THE HIDDEN

Lord Jesus Christ, how often I have said to You that I love You. I never stop long enough to ponder the deeper meaning behind those words. I never stop to examine if indeed I love You by faithfully following Your plan of salvation! Do I really keep my body under control so as to reflect the fact that I am Your disciple? Do I watch my thoughts turning myself and my ideas to Your greater ideas? Do I pray as You would have me to do so that my spirituality will be based on Your own spirituality?

I fully expect You to hear me whenever I call to You. I also expect You to answer me in the affirmative and to answer me according to my own time-line! I never stop long enough to figure out how You feel about things. Speak to me, O Lord.

"My son/daughter, did you ever stop to examine how difficult it is to communicate (and be understood in the way that is both honest and truthful) with so very many people, speaking different languages and from different cultures and drastically different socioeconomic backgrounds? You, My disciples, are the totality of your experiences: you are physically, psychologically, emotionally, culturally, theologically, sociologically and even economically the totality of all you have experienced, in those areas, throughout your individual lives! You are all unique! No two of you are alike! I must evaluate you as individuals, singular and special! You have had a great price paid for your salvation! Those events of Calvary were real. They were not simply figurative or fabricated, they happened and they were real! To this day, My disciples fail to understand that I want them to return My love for them.

In a relationship based on true love and friendship, the friends give and exchange a certain power over themselves to one another. When one hurts, the other hurts as well; when one is joyful, the other is joyful too: what affects the one automatically affects the other! When I came among you as Man, I was often hurt that My disciples didn't seem to understand this. They were not happy for Me that I wanted and needed to go to the Father. They seemed to resent My own needs and wanted Me to put their needs ahead of My needs. Lovers, true lovers, care for "the other" before they care for themselves! If I love you, and I do, I care most about your eternal salvation, after that and next, I care about your mental and emotional life; finally, I care about your physical health.

When so many of My disciples pray, they pray asking Me to physically heal them in the body. They seldom ask about spiritual healing or intellectual healing. Truth, authentic truth, is its own defense! If something is truthful and one can clearly see that it is true, one should be delighted to defend and welcome that truth. For example, if I know that my love for another is tainted, I must try to improve that love by submitting it to a higher power and asking the Power, Almighty God, to transfigure and transform my love into a greater love. So many disciples say they love one another while in reality, they lust for one another; they live together as "spouses" only to use one another for physical pleasure! They do this in direct violation of My Father's expressed will! They then expect My Father "to understand" and "to accept" this absolute violation of God's law. They excuse their conduct by saying they haven't hurt anyone!

When you love, ask yourself if you are conforming your life to God's expressed will! When a couple marry one another, they must agree on a common outlook on life or they will be in constant conflict with one another! Common interests, similar ideas, basic shared philosophy of life are the essential components for a healthy intimate relationship.

I want My own disciples to have a common healthy understanding of My Father's will. You have been made for eternity, not for this world. You have been made for God. God lives in your body, mind and spirit through Me. God is one with Me and nothing, absolutely nothing unclean, impure and sinful can ever hope to be incorporated into God without first being purged! You must be totally pure in body, mind and spirit to live in God; to touch God.

There is an attitude so prevalent in this latter part of the Twentieth Century which seeks to excuse evil by explaining it away. If I won't conform to the will of God, I'll make God's will conform to me! Once again, this kind of thinking comes from the spirit of evil, from the devil who seeks to invert reality making the Creator a creature, good into evil, love into hate! I must try to sort out the motives of each soul and all souls. I must see if there is authentic sincerity with the soul as that soul approaches Me for salvation.

You must spend time with Me and with My gospel. You must invest yourself and your energies in being alone in My Eucharistic Presence. You must pray and ponder My Presence in the Holy Eucharist if you are to ever understand My love. I gave you two great sacraments within three short days of each other: I gave you My Body, Blood, Soul and Divinity in the Eucharist, the Sacrifice of the Mass, on Holy Thursday, then, on Easter Sunday evening, I gave you the Sacrament of Reconciliation, of Penance!

I asked you to confess your sins so that My apostles could help you to correct them so you would sin no more. Through the power of the absolution, I, working in and through the Church, restore you to full communion of heart. "Cor ad cor loquitur": Heart speaks to heart. Your heart speaks to My heart and My heart speaks to your heart. This is the place where true lovers who are best and closest friends meet. This is, for us, the beginning of heaven."

Amen!

CONTEMPLATION – PRAYER

Jesus, I want to live within Your sacred heart, the living tabernacle of Your love. The immaculate heart of Your Holy Mother formed Your own heart, most sacred. She is the repository of Your Divine love, bursting through Your human nature! From Mary, in a purely human way, You learned how to love all mankind; from Mary, You experienced the human condition in all its imperfections, except for sin. Sinless, like Your Blessed Mother, You accepted all of the consequences of sin. You had to deal, interpersonally with the worst of us. You took those who denied You, those who doubted You, those who betrayed You, those who hurt You, and even those who sought to totally destroy You and transformed them – if only they would let You – into magnificent reflections of Yourself as Man.

Saul became Paul; Thomas, the doubter, became Thomas, the apostle, who gave his life for the faith; Simon the boastful, became Peter, the Rock; James and John, the arrogant, became humble, bold apostles giving their lives in service to the humble God who became Man! These are only a few of those closest to You. I think of Mary Magdalene out of whom You cast seven devils. She, the first called to deliver Your Easter message to Your apostles, became the most humble and innocent of Your redeemed! I think of the brave women – all of whom were at Your side on Calvary and saw Your total love! They never left You and, despite the risk, demonstrated to the whole world of that day, Your love and Your care! They were Your strength, Your encouragement, these holy women whose hiddenness is so complete that their names aren't even recorded in Holy Scripture! These and so many, many others found Your will, God's will, to be so complete and compelling that they gave their lives for the kingdom of God, Your saints, Your lovers!

Lord, so many of us see You as an "insurance policy" that we keep on a shelf until we need it. Our prayer, my prayer, consists of repeated bidding, constant asking for things to make my life easier, more physically and materially fulfilling and emotionally more comfortable. Why do I do this, Lord? That is not why You came to live among us. You came that we might have life and have it to the fullest. But, the kind of life You speak of is eternal life! You have told us that unless we deny ourselves, take up our crosses everyday and follow You, we cannot be Your disciples!

Lord, You alone know our hearts and You alone know how often we deny You and Your ways! You alone know that we are truly weak, truly arrogant and ever-unbending. Yet, O Lord, You pursue us, You never give up on us. Relentless Yourself, You are the all consuming Lover, the Hound of Heaven, who keeps us in His sights when we bolt this way and that way always trying to avoid Your loving gaze, Your call!

Lord, I do try to live close to You; yet, so many distractions from the world, the flesh and the devil compel me on in another way. Without Your help, without Your grace, I will never be able to resist so I can belong only to You, forever! I know that in heaven I will finally be free of temptations which lead me away from You and get me into compromising positions. I know that to choose to go to heaven, I absolutely must conform to Your grace. Your graces are helps which enable me to make the right choices in life. Your graces are all I need in this life to bring me safely home to my true eternal home in heaven. Give me, Lord, those actual graces which lead me to make the correct responses and choices and to live by them.

I know, dear Jesus, I am "wishy washie" and weak. I say one thing and do another. Courage, wisdom, compassion and moderation, the four virtues of the pagan philosopher Plato, I need to understand and I need to understand them in the light of Your Divine love, Lord Jesus Christ, in the light of Your gospel!

Give me the courage to face myself and all others and to stand for the values You teach me. Give me beauty and goodness, all virtues which will demonstrate to the world that I belong to You. Give me compassion for others. Help me to understand empathy and to practice it in my life. Lord, give the virtue of moderation, avoiding extremes which lead me into arrogance and pride; thinking I and only I am correct while others and their ways are wrong!

Help me, O Lord, to love with courage, wisdom, compassion and moderation all of my brothers and my sisters and especially those who do not know You or love You! When I am judged harshly and untruthfully, help me to try and understand why people see me in that light. If I have done anything to cause people to leave You and not to give You and Your values a second look, then Lord, help me to rid myself of it!

Lord, Your Vicar, Pope St. Pius X, at the beginning of the Twentieth Century (Sept. 8, 1907) wrote a strong warning to all of us living at the end of the twentieth century. His great letter, *Pascendi Dominici Gregis* (Feeding the Lord's Flock), tells us of that great evil, that great enemy of objective truth, which will rule and ruin so many hearts, that enemy called modernism, the denial of objective truth, the triumph of subjectivism.

In all of us and in each of us, there is this great tendency to deny objective truth. We only recognize what we want to recognize and only that. All other reality is compromised and goes unnoticed! In this totally self-centered and absolutely selfish world, there is room only for the self! People, places, events – even You, dear Lord – exist only for the ego's gratification in that philosophy of modernism, at once so wrong, so very evil and so all prevalent today!

Help me to overcome that evil, dear Lord. Help me to fully accept the central truths of Divine Revelation and to place my will at the disposal of God's holy will. Then I will know the true meaning of Your love. Then I will be ready for heaven and life in, with, and through You forever!

Amen!

HIS WILL IN MY LIFE

1. I will resist the call of today's culture to the philosophy of modernism. I will try to appreciate the objective presence of God in my life and I will conform my will to His will.

2. Love has as its essence the practice of "other-conscious" love. The "self-conscious" love of egotism has no real place in the God-love I am called to practice. It is this God-love that is lived in heaven. Lord, help me to practice God-love. Help me to live each and every day prepared to enter the Kingdom of God, my true home, my ultimate destiny.

3. Lord, help me to see You as my best Friend. Let me spend quality time with You; time that is non-distracted time. Let my mind, my thoughts, my desires only be in You, of You and exist for You. Lord, it is so difficult today to practice this kind of love. All too many of us are really absorbed totally in selfishness and egotism. Help me, O Lord, to make You the "Other" of my life and always to do Your great and holy will. All else will then take care of itself.

Amen!

CHAPTER EIGHT

*How Can I Love Like Jesus
Loved and Loves?
What Did Jesus Mean By Love?*

"When they had eaten their meal, Jesus said to Simon Peter, 'Simon, son of John, do you love (*agapè* = totally other-conscious, self-sacrificial love) Me, more than these?' 'Yes, Lord,' he said, 'You know that I love (*philia* = brotherly: "quid-pro-quo") You.' At which Jesus said, 'Feed My lambs.'

A second time Jesus put his question (to Simon), 'Simon, son of John, do you love (agapè = totally other-conscious, self-sacrificial love) Me? 'Yes, Lord,' Peter said,"You know that I love (philia = brotherly 'this-for-that' arranged love) You! Jesus replied, 'Tend My sheep.'

A third time Jesus asked him, 'Simon, son of John, do you love Me (*philia* = simply with an arranged kind of love, a 'this-for-that' arranged love). Peter was hurt because He had asked a third time, 'Do you love Me?' So he said to Jesus, 'Lord, You know everything. You know well that I love (philia) You.' Jesus said to him, 'Feed My sheep.'

I tell you solemnly; as a young man you fastened your belt and went about as you pleased; but when you are older you will stretch out your hands, and another will tie you fast, and carry you off against your will! (What He said indicated the sort of death by which Peter was to glorify God.) When Jesus had finished speaking He said to him, 'Follow Me.'" (John 21:15-19).

One cannot cite the First Letter of St. Paul to the Corinthian Church which speaks about love, without first explaining the wonderful conclusion of John's gospel! The time, the circumstances, the two people involved and the topic to which the concept of love is applied speak eloquently to what we Christians are all about.

Jesus and Peter are speaking their final words together before the ascension of the Lord into heaven. Much clarification and "clearing the air" needs to be done. Peter, always mercurial, up and down like a child's "yo yo" toy, now had to face his Lord. No doubt words of past empty boasting about his loyalty, his bravery, his fidelity haunted him as, alone with the Master, Peter's "other-self," the human Simon, Son of John, now naked in the high noon day sun, fully exposed for what he should have been and often bragged to be but never was, is for all the world to see absolutely exposed!

I have often wondered how the event described ever got into the gospel narrative! Since only Jesus and Peter were present – at least within hearing distance – Peter must have told the story on himself! If I'm not mistaken, I can remember from seminary days, that Peter often told revealing, humiliating stories about himself, "thought and/or so taught" my Scripture professor!

Note that Jesus speaks of this totally "other-conscious" love, this agapè, in terms of the new-priesthood that He (Jesus) establishes! Feeding the sheep and tending to the lambs is the field in which the agapè love is to be practiced! Often, we, in today's culture, think of agapè love in terms of male-female love, the love of husband and wife or the love of father and son, mother and daughter, etc. That is certainly one expression; however, here, Our Lord speaks of a wider far more expansive object of the agapè love, all the sheep. All the sheep, all the lambs are to be fed and cared for by Peter, the vicar of Christ and Bishop of the Catholic Church.

A close examination of the Lord's use of the "sheep image" will open many doors to us, especially in the light of absolutely "other-conscious" Christ-like love! I call your attention to John 20:1-18, the beautiful teaching on the role of the good shepherd. Recognition by the sheep of the shepherd is the focus of the first section. Jesus explains how the shepherd is to act with the sheep and how the sheep are to respond to the shepherd. He teaches how the good shepherd will lay down his life for the sheep. Shepherd and sheep have a totally dependent relationship and now Jesus Christ insists that the shepherd must love his sheep and lambs and care for them with agapè love! Very different, indeed!

In today's culture we are exclusive of our possessions! We are not inclusive! Even in the world of advertising I see a fundamental change: television and radio commercials used to dwell on inclusion. People would purchase a product and invite friends and neighbors to enjoy the product. Today, we are moving – and in many ways have moved away from – inclusion to exclusion! We are happy that we have the "one and only" of a product. We are happy to have been in competition with our neighbor and to have beaten our neighbor to the desired goal! Exclusion has replaced inclusion as the tone and theme of the desired good! How terribly sad, how totally anti-Christian! Anti-agapè love!

Love is the most confused word in our culture today. We really think we know what it means but haven't – in reality – got the slightest "clue" as to love's true meaning!

Junk TV has a wider listening, viewing audience than any other form of entertainment. On Junk TV people enjoy seeing people hurting people. In what way is this different from what the ancient pagans did when they threw people to the wild beasts, crucified and tortured them, confiscated their property, etc., etc.? It is not different. It's worse! Exploitation of one another seems to be the rule of the day and growing!

Juxtaposed against this model of apagè "the ideal," Jesus Christ breaks upon the universal scene with a new kind of love, lived in very new kinds of ways and always inclusive of the neighbor. This love, this agapè, is absolutely the same kind of love that an anxiously awaiting pregnant couple have for their newborn child at the time of the baby's birth!

It is marked by total, all-consuming love. It is a love that is fully focused on the beloved. It is a love that would die so that the beloved could live a quality life! Jesus insists that this is the quality of love that His priests must have and demonstrate or show to all the sheep and lambs. He insists that this agapè love must also be the kind and quality of love that the sheep and lambs have for one another!

When I think of sheep, my mind travels to Europe where I had an opportunity to study many years ago. Often, I would see the Scottish shepherd tending the sheep and I wondered how he could ever get the sheep to hear his voice. Scattered over acres of mountains, they (the sheep and lambs) were marked on their coats, with bright blue, yellow or red dye. To my amazement, the shepherd would call and the sheep would come running. I thought: when I hear the Lord call do I come running? Most of us don't, I think.

So many of us are exclusive of opportunities for virtue. We actually resist them, avoid them, see them as being too bothersome! We are, however, very inclusive of opportunities for vice! Temptations are resolved by giving into them, by justifying them, making them a part of my life. I truly believe we resolve guilt by avoiding it! We don't spend time to face our legitimate guilt and we get rid of all opportunities to bring it into our consciousness! In The Handbook of Family Psychology and Therapy, Vol. 1, the authors discuss the various types of love which, they state from their perspective, "appear to fit the different levels of ego development." They identified six levels. They are:

1. Mania ...: the person is obsessed with the loved one, possessive, intensely dependent, irrationally jealous, and unable to tolerate the thought of loss of the loved one. This kind of love, associated with low self-esteem and a poor self-

concept, is probably typical of persons at the impulsive/self-protective level of ego development.

2. Ludus ...: The lover is a self-centered game player who plays to get the greatest reward for the least cost and who hates dependency on self or others. This description appears to fit the kind of love relationship that a person at the self protection stage would develop.

3. Pragma ...: The lover is practical, sensible, keenly aware of, and realistic about, what can be expected from the relationship and what it is likely to cost, and forms or breaks up a relationship for practical reasons. This kind of relationship also has characteristics of the self-protective stage, but the capacity to assess realistically the pluses and minuses from the mate's point of view indicates some progression beyond the self-protective stage. Because this description contains elements of the conformist stage, perhaps we should place the person who develops this kind of love at the self-protective/conformist level.

4. Eros ...: In eros, or romantic love, the lover is idealized, the relationship is idealized, and the person is preoccupied with pleasing the beloved. The idealization of, and concern about, the other is typical of the conformist stage.

5. Storge ...: Rapport, interdependency, self-disclosure, mutual need fulfillment, and a long-term commitment to the relationship are characteristic ... (it) is more typical of long-time, intimate friends ... (as in) an old, happily married couple.

6. Agapè ...: The lover is caring, promotes the best for the beloved, and gives without expectation of, or necessity for, return from the other ... Agapè is not the kind of love that is likely in two young lovers ... (it) might be found in an Agapè, love, that is Christ-centered, Christ-rooted, Christ-

destiny love is, by the professional psychological standard, almost impossible to achieve; yet, Christ Jesus tells Simon Peter and, through him, all of us, that we must have this "almost impossible to achieve" love for one another! Is the Lord mad? How can this agapè be achieved?

There is only one answer; that answer is simple: What is impossible for man is possible with God! If Christ is really living within us and, hence, the kingdom of God is within us, then it is possible with, through, and solely because of God that attainment of agapè love is possible and, yes, even totally expected by God of true authentic disciples of Jesus Christ.

That is precisely why we cannot speak of our relationship with Jesus Christ as "my religion" or "my Church" or even, "my faith." What we need to do is to rethink our relationship with Jesus Christ as just that: a quality relationship based on agapè interpersonal factors! In other words, we are lovers! Lovers care for each other; lovers need each other; lovers treat each other with great respect and with enormous sensitivity! Lovers always speak to and with each other; lovers "take incoming calls" from each other and hear with both ears what the other says and does not say!

It is absolutely impossible to love Jesus in this way without taking quality time to be with Him. We must be with Him according to the ways outlined in the previous chapters. We must pray to the Lord and continually submit our finite (limited) wills to His infinite will. In the sacraments, we will greet our Divine Lover who eternally awaits us. In our contemplation, freed from the guilt of sin, we will know Him and our knowledge will grow greater and greater of God and the ways of God. Each encounter will draw us closer and closer into the sacred heart of Jesus and the immaculate heart of Mary. We will be changed people, transfigured people who will really be ready, a heart-beat from now to enter heaven.

Amen!

THE UNSPOKEN, THE HIDDEN

"Lord Jesus Christ, my Brother, my closest Friend, my only true Companion in this life, speak to me of Your hidden, unspoken love and all You endured for me." Speak, Lord Jesus Christ:

"I loved you long before you were conceived. Don't try to figure it out, the angels couldn't figure it out or explain it. My Father created you in the image of God. He called creation into existence for you. He gave you free will and the ability to say 'yes' or 'no' to His will. My Father's love is God-love. God is love and the person who lives in God lives in God-love and God-love lives in that person.

From the psychologists, you know how nearly impossible God-love (agapè) is to achieve, even impossible between most older spouses! Face it, agapè love is impossible because it takes too much work, it costs too much of any person. Impossible, yes, from a human perspective, but not from God's perspective! The laborers build in vain unless the Lord builds the house; the guards guard the city in vain unless the Lord keeps the vigil; unless the Lord keeps the watch.

I often think of the many conversations the Father and I had long before the world was created. I told you and I told My people that 'before Abraham came to be, I am'! (cf. John 8:58). What did you think I meant by that remark? Do you remember when I told you that the Son of God cannot do anything by Himself – He can only do what He sees the Father doing. For whatever the Father does, the Son does likewise. You own My life's story. If you want to know the relationship between the Father and the Son, read John 5: 20-47!

Do you remember Me telling you that other disciples were murmuring in protest at what I said was My relationship with My Father and how I planned to be with you down through the corridors of time, language differences and cultural uniqueness? I told you that My flesh was food indeed and My blood was drink indeed and that he who feeds on My flesh and drinks My blood has eternal life and (that) I will raise him up on the last day ... I said that the man who feeds on My flesh and drinks My blood remains in Me, and I in him ... the man who feeds on this (Eucharistic) Bread shall live forever. (cf. John 6:54-58). I began this teaching by insisting that he who does not eat the Flesh of the Son of Man and drink His Blood (will have) no life in himself. (cf. John 6:53). I don't think I could have been clearer! Do you think that I could have been clearer in what I asked of My disciples?

When a person gives himself to another, that is a great gift. When God the Son lowers Himself to become a Man, that is truly the greatest gift. When the God-man becomes a piece of what appears to be bread and a draft of what looks like wine, that is agapè, God-love at its best! It is only by means of this God-love that you can enter heaven. It is the "bridge" between heaven and earth. It is the final gift of My love for you! Please, listen to Me and gift Me with your love."

Amen!

CONTEMPLATION – PRAYER

Lost in contemplation, the great St. Thomas Aquinas
     prayed:
"O hidden Godhead, humbly I adore You
truly hidden beneath these appearances
(of bread and wine).
To You I bow my heart and bend my
knee since contemplating You
all fails for me.
The senses: sight, touch, taste in You
are all deceived, faith-heard through
the ear – is only to be believed!
I firmly hold to whatever God's only
Son has spoken ... than truth's own
Word, there simply is nothing more true.
You see, God only on the Cross was
hidden from view ... but here in
the Eucharist, hides Deity and manhood too!
Lord, I in both professing firm belief,
make my own prayer that of Dismas,
the repentant thief.
Lord, Your wounds as Thomas Your doubting
apostle saw, I do not see ...
Yet, You confess my Lord and God to be!
My faith, dear Lord confirm and my
childlike trust impart and may
I love You, O Lord, my God with all my heart.
O blessed memorial of Our Lord's own dying.
O living bread to mortal's life supplying ...
Become indeed the life of my own mind
so that in You, I may my satisfaction find.

O Pelican, mother Pelican, self-wounding
on the cross, me – unclean man – yet
cleansed with Your own blood, of which
a single drop for sinners spilled,
can purge this wicked world of all its guilt.
O Jesus whom at present in the Holy Eucharist
veiled I see, what I so thirst for,
Grant to me: that I may see Your blessed self unfolding
and may find my rest forever – Your glory in beholding."

- Adoro Te Devote, St. Thomas Aquinas
translation: Msgr. Jeremiah F. Kenney.

"Lord, as I contemplate this great prayer of Your Church's doctor and priest, Thomas Aquinas, I see hidden in its beautiful words and marvelous images, the fullness of Your agapè, Your totally other-conscious love for me. You are that great mother Pelican who in the hardness and cold-ness of the winter, pecks a hole in its breast to feed its young with its own blood; Lord, You are the greatest Lover and the most magnificent Friend one could ever have. You never leave us! We leave You! We wander far away from You and stay far away until You find us. We are the lost sheep whose independence causes You such great pain and, when found, give You such great joy.

In doing Your will, Lord, will we truly find our peace? In becoming living reflections of Your ways will we find the way home to heaven? We are all grains of seed and we really must die if the plant is to grow! Help me, Jesus, to trust in You! You trusted in me, dear Lord, and I never ceased to let You down. I always think only of myself and my ways. Your ways are put in the background – and considered often last and only when convenient!

Lord, teach me how to love You as You love me! Lord, help me not to be so needy of approval from others. It is this need of approval which brings me to a sense of my own worthlessness. Help me, dear Lord, to understand that there are three things I must do with You alone: With You, I am born; with You, I must love; with You, I must die! Lord, let me review the great prayer of the Saint, Thomas Aquinas, his *Adoro Te Devote*. Let me make it my own prayer, my own devotion and my eternal worship."

Amen!

HIS WILL IN MY LIFE

1. Jesus, help me to be agapè love for You and for my loved ones. Help me to practice this love each and every day.

2. Jesus, You know how "alone" and lonely it is to be a faithful disciple; yet, You call each of us to have that special, unique relationship with You. You want us to "travel" down through the corridors of time and cultural differences to get to know You and to love You. You are for each of us and for all of us the "true other" in our lives; You are that one without whom we could never know truly how to love!

3. Jesus let me love my sisters and my brothers as You love them. Help me to see beyond their sins to the beautiful creation each is, made in God's image and likeness.

4. Lord, help me to love Your Holy Eucharist and to be "eucharist" for my brothers and for my sisters. Lord Jesus, I love You! Teach me to love You more and more!

Amen!

CHAPTER NINE

*HOW CAN I BECOME A TRUE
"RELATIVE" OF JESUS?
IS MARY, THE MOTHER OF JESUS,
REALLY MY OWN MOTHER IN HEAVEN?
WHAT CAN MARY TEACH ME ABOUT
BEING A GOOD SON/DAUGHTER?*

Newsweek, one of our most popular weekly magazines, in their August 25, 1997 edition, carried an article entitled, "Hail, Mary." Kenneth L. Woodward is given credit for the article with Andrew Murr, Christopher Dickey, Sarah Van Boven and Hersch Doby all making their contribution. The focus of the article, as one might suspect, is the Mother of Jesus, Mary of Nazareth, and what, at that time, could have been a possible new dogma pronounced by the pope calling Mary "Co-Redemptrix, Mediatrix of All Graces and Advocate for the People of God."

At the time, debate was hot and heavy that the Blessed Virgin, rather than a focus of unity within the body of Christ, among God's holy people, could well have become a source of disunity, even within the Catholic Church, because of possible or probable papal action!

What always troubled me is the popular argument or attitude that it is within the power of the pope to do anything he wants to do to make happen anything he wants to make happen in theology or mariology! If Mary were not what the various titles say she really is, then no pronouncement of any pope could make them be such! That's the point! If the reality did not already exist, then the pope could never pronounce it to exist!

There is an old rule of law: *nemo dat quod non habet*, you cannot give what you do not have! Simply put, the Holy Father cannot declare anything he wants to declare as dogma. He cannot make or break something which is not within truth to do. Whatever this pope or any future pope may decide on this issue or any other issue, will be heavily determined by the Holy Spirit of God and how that same Holy Spirit chooses to guard, guide and direct the Church.

The mere fact that the Christian world is having this discussion is itself a testimony to the singular, closest to the

Lord, and most significant human being in the life of Jesus Christ and to the life of each of us who calls himself/herself a disciple of Jesus Christ! The Blessed Virgin Mary of Nazareth, called in the Council of Ephesus (431 A.D.), the Mother of God, has been for hundreds of years both the source of Christian unity and, some say, the cause of alienation of one Christian body from another.

The Vatican newspaper, *L'Osservatore Romano*, published in English, here in Baltimore, Maryland, has seen this Holy Father routinely and continually call Mary, Advocate and Mediatrix. He even said that it "was fitting" that Jesus would have appeared first to Our Lady, His own Mother, following His resurrection from the dead." I personally have believed this from my first days as a young religious brother of the Congregation of Holy Cross. This is based on an old scholastic rule: "*potuit, decuit, fecit*": He had the power to and could do it; (in justice); it was certainly fitting for Him to do it, and He did it!

I have often asked myself what I would do in similar circumstances. I loved my own mother very much. I was devoted to her. I think if, for any reason, my mother had to experience what Mary of Nazareth, the Mother of Jesus, experienced, and I had the ability to relieve her of some stress caused by the various events, so horrible to even speak of, I would go first to my mother in order to bring to her a sense of peace and joy. It is the only charitable thing to do. Not to do this, logically, would be almost impossible to justify. Any devoted person would do this for the person he/she loved most in the world.

Certainly, if a Christian man or woman adopts the attitude that they don't care or the attitude, the "shrug-of-the-shoulder" approach resulting in "summary dismissal," there is no room for argument let alone discussion! People do seem to feel this way about Our Lady. They either enthrone her in their heart of hearts or cast her aside as insignificant!

The argument that is cited in the first chapter of this book, the argument that God needed Mary's "yes" to redeem us, seems to me to speak to how this author feels and what he believes on the topic. Mary showed us the way of submission to God's holy will! Nothing is ever lacking in the sacrifice of Jesus on Calvary; but, we needed to be shown by one of ourselves how to apply the merits of the death of the Lord to ourselves in the here and now! We needed Mary's example, her faith, her love, her risk, her Jesus to make redemption happen!

Again and again, Jesus calls us His brothers and sisters; we are truly His great mystical Body, His Church. This entire book is filled with Scriptural quotes attesting to this fact; but, once again, I think we are in the position of not being "able to see the forest for the trees" if we hold that we don't need Mary. Without Mary, there would be no Jesus! Without Jesus and His cross, there would be no heaven for us! There is, in my opinion, no getting around it. They come as a package: you can't have one without the other! Mary and Jesus; Jesus and Mary!

Several years ago I was at the bedside of a dying man who had left the priesthood. He was dying and he knew it. Before "final confusion" had set in he began to talk. (I'm sure he wouldn't object to this sharing of his thoughts.) The man had spent years struggling with celibacy, its expectations, its demands. He found purity to be a life-long struggle. He had been unfaithful but he never ceased praying to Mary, to Our Lady, to help him. He attempted marriage twice, both relationships failed and his journey in life ended with painful cancer compounded with heart problems.

He told me he never missed saying the daily rosary. He

told me that his first wife hated things Christian and wouldn't permit any religious symbols in their home. He wouldn't dare to own a rosary, let alone bring it in the house. He said he took the chain that was on the bathtub drain stopper in their old-fashioned home and used to pray the beads while taking a bath! He never missed!

When I saw him it was about eight days before his death. He was able to be reconciled by Our Lady who – in his life – played a most important role, that of "helper-unique" to the Redeemer of that troubled priest!

Today, there are as many opinions as there are mouths to speak them! Our own prejudices get in the way of really separating emotion from issue and we take positions on topics so sacred, so remote, so unique and so beyond our understanding. Do we truly believe, all things being equal, that Almighty God would deny His immaculate Mother any title when He gives us, miserable as we are, the wonders of the world of Divine graces? Would we deny our mothers?

We are all looking for a "measuring stick" against which to determine if we should give titles for the Mother of the Messiah to the Blessed Virgin Mary! How dare we do such a thing! When the archangel Gabriel spoke to her he spoke in quiet eloquence and glorious entitlement! We saw what happened to the father of John the Baptist when he dared to voice his opinion and doubt on such a lofty divine decision! What we need on this issue, as on so many others, is to trust in Jesus that He will do what is best for the greatest human love of His life, His own Blessed Mother.

Often, in my life as, I'm sure, in the lives of most of you, whenever your mother asked a favor of you, if it were within your power to give the favor, you would do it. I know I could never refuse my own mother or father anything either one asked. In fact, if the truth be known, I would anticipate their requests by doing what I knew they were going to ask before they asked! I remember that my parents were concerned that their grandchildren be given a Catholic secondary school education. I had been the founding dean of the Catholic boys' school in my home town. Even before they asked me to do what I could to "pave the way" for the boys to be accepted as students at the school, I had spoken to some of my former classmates on behalf of my nephews. They were all good students so they really didn't need my help, but to please my parents and to "do for my own family" I did whatever I could.

In God's family, it is no different. Mary raised Jesus, we are His sisters and brothers in the order of Grace, hence we are Mary's children in that order. Whatever be the opinion of a person on the various events at Fatima, Lourdes, Guadalupe, etc., the fact remains that Mary continues to warn us, to offer us correction for our misdeeds, to encourage us to pray and to bring us that constant message that she is praying to God the Son on our behalf. In all of her appearances recognized by the church, Mary, when she speaks, speaks about her Son, Jesus Christ. She speaks about her constant request of Him to forgive us for what we have done against the will of God. In 1854, Pope Pius IX defined Mary's Immaculate Conception. He said that by virtue of a special grace of God and in view of her being the Mother of Christ, the Virgin Mary was preserved from original sin. At Lourdes, in 1858, Mary appeared 18 times between February and July and called herself, "the Immaculate Conception." Pope Leo XIII designated February 11 a feast day for this and Pope St. Pius X made it universal in 1907.

Clearly, Mary's role is singular! It is the only one of its kind in human nature. Mary's role is to raise each of us to be her sons and daughters in grace. She wants us to get to heaven, she cannot bear the loss of any one of us. She needs us to be her faithful children. She is our Mother, our human nature's solitary boast. If then we belong to Jesus we also belong to Mary. She is my heavenly Mother; God's chosen and given way to Jesus. To Jesus through Mary! Trust Jesus, He is God's Son and Mary's too!

Amen!

THE UNSPOKEN – THE HIDDEN

Mary's Eyes

An angel's song was all the strength she had
        to keep moving along ... that dark, rough
And dangerous way ...
An old lady's greeting, manifesting and fleeting
        as she pondered what manner indeed was
        this meeting!
'Hail full of grace, my pregnancy's pace, leapt
        for joy -
As I heard your Choice, lovingly carried
        within your voice.
You came to me from out of the night,
        a long hard road you traversed, so cold.
You took no account of killers, rapists
        or thieves to give yourself to alleviate
        my needs ...
So that our babies might meet and call us
        to know, that God, the Almighty, would
Manifest and show – His Presence, His total love,
        His only Son from heaven alone!

Three long months you washed, cared and cleaned,
        to keep me, my husband and kin
Comfortable, warm and from getting too thin!
No one knew the Treasure you carried within,
No one could imagine that God of our dreams one day
        a seamless garment would give to redeem
A poor human race, so callous and so cold
Because of what so long ago you were mercifully told!

That request of great Gabriel, changed our life's direc-
    tion,
Due only to your ever gentle suggestion:
"How can this be, since I do not know man?"
Great Gabriel gave you the explanation,
Still you did offer your own supplication:
"Be it done unto me according to your Word."'

For ages untold, long awaited by all of the nations,
Came at your word from earth's many stations!
At whose great Name every knee shall bend ...
In heaven above and at earth's distant end!

You carried Him close unto your breast,
And you fed Him gently in Joseph's loving nest!
You two brought Him, ever so tender and young,
To the great Temple in the City of Jerusalem!
There a man and a woman both ancient of days ...
Upon their arms gently learned of His holy ways:
"Dismiss Your servant, O ancient of Days
My old eyes have beheld the glory of Your Ways!"
Your heart, O Mother, so young and so frail,
Would soon be pierced by earth's toughest gales!
Pierced by swords ever so cruel ...
You would learn the meaning of this symbolic Tool!
The tongue, that rudder so small, would struggle
The ship to steer to life's selfish call.
Still your ways, so selfless and kind, always and
Forever so lovingly good ...
Couldn't steer Him away from that terrible wood!

A carpenter's life did He choose to live,
Always a life, forever, all ages to give.

To king and pauper, to slave and free, to one and to all
   eternally ...
To Pilate's cross, washed hands could not clean,
You made your own, Jesus, so selfless and keen!
Little Mother, you traveled ever so near, your Jesus so
   dear.
He was your Son, your only One!

When at last, O Mary, you lost Him
   in the Temple's precinct,
You and Joseph did find Him, who is God's own link!
You wondered, pondered and thought until;
At Cana's wedding feast, no more wine was to be had
Making host and hostess ever so sad.
"Whatever He tells you, indeed you will do;"
So very few did notice and knew
That at your word and in obedience to you, Mary,
The Almighty, that God-Man did suddenly
   break-through!
From water to wine; from earth to heaven;
From fallen humanity to a people redeemed ...
So wonderful, so extraordinary and so it surely seemed
O Mary, for it was at your unspoken command
That God, the Almighty, heard the cry of our stand!
You always did notice our needs before all else ...
You call us to relinquish our very own self.
Yes, Mary, He who hears of your gentle call,
Truly, truly will He stand ever so tall!
Never will he or she ever again take a fall,
For sin and evil are broken once and for all!
Because of you, Mary, we have a heavenly call ...
The First, the Last, bids us to stand tall!
Jesus, the Alpha, the Omega, and all that is good,

Who for us did die upon that rough wood,
Will call us one day to heaven above ...
Where forever we will sing of His gentle love ...
For one and for all ... who stand so straight and so tall,
To hear the Father's voice so lovingly call:
"Come home, come here, let Me hold you, My all,
My son, My daughter, you always hear of My call!
Into the hollow of My hands I hold you:
The short and the tall ...
In My great arms forever will you live,
Because to so many you always did give ...
Never, never to fear ... yes, My love, heaven now is here!"

- Msgr. Jeremiah F. Kenney, 1998

Thank Mary for Jesus; thank Jesus for Mary! Together they incorporated us into their family.

I really believe that at the end of time we really will get a new body to "house" our souls and spirits. Until then, I think the eternal Christ, in the human body (risen, ascended in glory) and human soul – His full manhood, will keep our own souls and spirits "housed." That is why we must struggle to rid ourselves of sin in order that we may be free to touch God.

No sin, no evil could ever be incorporated into the glorified human nature of Christ. We must spend time getting rid of those items in our lives that get in the way of the flowing rivers of God's grace. Mary can be of enormous help to us. She loves being hidden! She watches us as our own mothers watched over us. More so than our own biological parents, Mary's knowledge of the eternal value of each person is second only to that of God. Mary will crush the head of Satan to win a soul for her Son.

Today, we speak of justification of personhood. Seldom, if ever, do we call anything a sin. Our philosophy of integration of good and evil "waters-down" (dilutes) the truly good. Mary calls us to reject this lukewarmness. She calls us to be on fire with God's own love. She constantly reminds us to fight for what is right, for what is God's holy will. Mary is our Mother who will show us the Father's home. Mary, after all, gave us Jesus, our Brother.

Amen!

CONTEMPLATION – PRAYER

Mary, my Mother, teach me about Jesus. What was it like to feel Him forming within you? What was it like to give Him birth? The angelic doctor, St. Thomas Aquinas, said: "As the sun penetrates glass, so of Mary, Jesus Christ was born!" Mary, did you sense at the birth of Jesus, the presence of God? Did you hear, together with the shepherds, the angel's song? Will heaven's life allow me one day, in that eternity, to replay His birth in that stable so cold? I want so very much to get to know you, to have you be my best friend and my Mom!

So many of us never pay you any mind; yet, for so very many years you cared for the God-man. You changed Him, you clothed Him, fed Him, and housed Him; you taught Him and healed Him when He became weak; you spoke of Him to your neighbors and loved Him when He excelled. Your life was within His life and as He increased, you sought to decrease.

With St. Joseph, you struggled to earn a wage so that He could live a normal healthy life, interacting with His peers. You wanted Him to be humble and taught God the virtue of humility! It is not by accident that you seldom did speak, because you were and ever are, the "all loving listener" who hears our cries, our calls in the loneliness of the long night. You heard Him when first He spoke and you even taught Him to walk, catching Him lest He fall. Dearest Mother, He was your whole life, your reason for being. You must have followed Him throughout His public ministry. Whenever we see you in Scripture, you are always with the holy women: never talking, always present, always listening. Did you ever try to speak with your Jesus as He traveled on and along the roads of His country? You must have. How do we know? We remember His words from Calvary's cross: "Seeing his mother there with the disciple whom He loved, Jesus said to His mother, 'Woman, there is your son.'" In turn He said to the disciple, 'There is your mother.' From that hour onward, the disciple took her into his care." (John 19:26-27).

How often we have looked at these words and missed the full impact of their meaning! "From that hour onward. ..." Where did Mary live before that hour? She must have lived with Jesus. She never left His side! Jesus died and minutes before He died, He gave His beloved disciple the care of His mother. He gave her to John as if she were John's own biological mother. Through John, calling her "Woman," Jesus gives Mary to each one of us! Jesus knows how deeply we need you, O Mary. You cared for Jesus, now you will care for John who is so like Jesus.

Of all the apostles, the beloved disciple, in his goodness, in his courage, in his lifestyle and in his love, most resembled your Jesus! Your care for John mirrored your care and love for Jesus.

Loving Mother, care for us; raise us; look after our eternal needs. Never let us be separated from Jesus. Did John comfort you as you longed to be with Jesus? Was John there at your dormition? Did he witness your assumption into heaven?

What was it like to see your Jesus again after His resurrection? Since you were with His apostles and since they saw Him frequently, did you see Him, too? Of course you did! They would never have left you alone. Where would you have gone but with brave John, your Son's gift to you? John had to be with the others and, therefore, you had to be with them as well.

Did you see Him alone, just the two of you, Jesus and Mary, together, following His resurrection and throughout the 40 days? Your heart must have longed to ascend with Him as He rose to join the eternal Father.

Dearest Mother, how long after the Lord's ascension did you live with us here on earth? I have no doubt that the apostles, the holy women, the other disciples must have cared for you, listened to you as you told them those stories of the Incarnation, the Nativity, the flight into Egypt, the presentation in the Temple, the finding of the Child in the Temple, etc., etc.

Did your beautiful eyes fill with tears as you recalled the words of Simeon. "This child is destined to be the downfall and the rise of many in Israel, a sign that will be opposed – and you yourself shall be pierced with a sword – so that the thoughts of many hearts may be laid bare." (Luke 2: 34b-35). How often did you ponder those words? Have you since then, even today, continued to "ponder" them, Blessed Mother?

We need so very much to see your eyes, we need to feel your pain; we need to walk in your shoes; we need to know, love and serve Jesus as you do, today, yesterday and always! Heart of Mary, make my heart live inside of your immaculate heart!

Amen!

HIS WILL IN MY LIFE

1. I will care and treasure Mary, as John, the Beloved, cared and treasured her. I will never permit anyone to speak ill of her or diminish her role in salvation history.

2. I will pray Mary's rosary each and every day. I will pray it slowly and meditate on the words and/or mysteries of the rosary.

3. I will see myself as I really am, a child of Mary, totally united to Jesus and to the countless numbers of people who have died; people living on earth and people yet unborn! Jesus is all-in-all to each and every one, even to those who do not know it!

4. I will try to say this little prayer each and every day as often as I can:

My Mother, Jesus gave you to me.
Raise me as you raised Jesus.
Never leave me now; be with me when I die.
Amen!

CHAPTER TEN

CAN I EVER GO BACK TO CALVARY
TO SEE WHAT REALLY HAPPENED
AT THE TIME JESUS CHRIST DIED?
CAN I LEARN SOMETHING FROM HOW AND WHY
JESUS SUFFERED AND DIED?

"Then Pilate took Jesus and scourged Him. And the soldiers impaled a crown of thorns, and put it on His head, and arrayed Him in a purple robe, they came up to Him, saying, 'Hail, King of the Jews!' and struck Him with their hands. Pilate went out again, and said to them (the people), 'Behold, I am bringing Him (Jesus) out to you, that you may know that I find no crime in Him.' So Jesus came out, wearing the crown of thorns and the purple robe. Pilate said to the crowd, 'Here is the man'! When the chief priests and officers saw Him, they cried out, 'Crucify Him, crucify Him!' Pilate said to them, 'Take Him yourselves and crucify Him, for I find no crime in Him.' The Jews answered him, 'We have a law, and by that law He ought to die, because He had made Himself the Son of God.'

When Pilate heard these words, he was the more afraid; he entered the praetorium again and said to Jesus, 'Where are You from?' But Jesus gave no answer. Pilate, therefore, said to Him, 'You will not speak to me? Do You not know that I have power to release You, and power to crucify You?' Jesus answered him, 'You would have no power over Me unless it had been given you from above; therefore, he who delivered Me to you has the greater sin. ...' (Pilate) said to the Jews, 'Here is your king!' They cried out, 'Away with Him, away with Him, crucify Him! Pilate said to them, 'Shall I crucify your King?' The chief priests answered, 'We have no king but Caesar.' Then he (Pilate) handed Him over to them to be crucified.

So they took Jesus, and He went out, bearing His own cross, to the place called the place of the skull, which is called in Hebrew, Golgotha. There they crucified Him, and with Him two others, one on either side, and Jesus between them ...

When the soldiers had crucified Jesus they took His

garments and made four parts, one for each soldier; also His tunic. But the tunic was without seam, woven from top to bottom; so they said 'Let us not tear it, but cast lots for it to see whose it shall be.'

So the soldiers did this. But standing by the cross of Jesus were His mother, and His mother's sister, Mary the wife of Clopas, and Mary Magdalene. When Jesus saw His mother, and the disciple whom He loved standing near, He said to His mother, 'Woman, behold your son!' Then He said to the disciple, 'Behold, your mother!' And from that hour the disciple took her to his own home.

After this, Jesus, knowing that all was now finished, said (to fulfill the scripture), 'I thirst.' A bowl full of vinegar stood there, so they put a sponge full of vinegar on hyssop and held it to His mouth. When Jesus had received the vinegar, He said, 'It is finished'; and He bowed His head and gave up His spirit." (John 19:1-11; 14b-18; 23-24a; 28-30).

The purpose of the "Roman method" of putting someone to death was solely to teach a lesson to the crowds. In addition to physical, mental and emotional torture, the Romans were world masters of a slow and painful death. The purpose was also to scare and terrify the people into following the rules ... or else!

Scourging was masterfully done. In over 40 years of religious or priestly life, I think I have read my share of texts on the passion of the Lord. Some are better than others but most generally agree on the following points:

• The severe scourgings was done to totally shock the crowd and render the victim a cripple for life. In itself, it often resulted in the prolonged agony and death of the victim. Small "iron bar bell-like" and very rough metal was sewn onto leather straps. The straps had 12 to 15 individual straps bound together into a handle. Two experts (scourgers) were to scourge by standing on either side of the victim who was tied to a column. He was totally stripped naked. One scourger would apply the scourge to the back and "rip" the scourge straps away so as to flay the skin from the body. The entire back from below the head to the feet was scourged. Naturally, infection would set in. In some severe scourgings, the person was scourged on the chest and legs as well. Usually, the scourging was meant to be the full penalty of the crime committed. That is why Pilate ordered Jesus to be scourged. He thought they would accept that and not demand the other, i.e., crucifixion. Some studies I have made reveal that crucifixion never took place following the severe scourging. The scourged person would be entirely too weak to walk let alone to carry a cross or cross-beam. Jesus was also crowned with thorns! This wasn't done to others. It grew out of the hatred of the Roman soldiers for the Jews of the time. Palestine was a terrible assignment for the Roman soldier. There were countless rebellions and many assassinations of foreign soldiers by the population. Most people in authority resented being assigned to the area and were happy to have their time in and go home as soon as possible!

At the point of the Lord having to carry the cross, Jesus had been crowned with large thorns and had been scourged from head to foot! He was unique in having suffered more than any known "criminal" of His day.

The "art" of crucifixion was horrible. Large spikes were driven into the wrists and feet. A "seat" was sometimes fixed to the cross and contained a large spike to insure the victim wouldn't move. The victim often "sat" on the spike. He was naked. Ropes were sometimes used to "hold" the victim onto the cross so that the weight of the victim's body wouldn't tear itself from the cross!

The victim died by means of suffocation! His lungs filled up slowly and death was the only welcome relief he could hope to have.

• Jesus Christ underwent all of the various forms of torture employed by the Romans. The humiliation began when the cries of the previous Sunday's "Hosannas" turned into shouts of "crucify Him, crucify Him." Even Pilate, perhaps at first not meaning to order His death, having had Jesus scourged, compounded the torture beyond what the crowds had demanded. Jesus Christ was, in my opinion, the most tortured Victim in the history of Roman conquest!

• We must now consider that Jesus Christ, a Man, was/is also God the Son, the Second Divine Person of the Blessed Trinity! Given this, He suffered far more from any pain or torture than any other human ever could have suffered. In addition to the denial, betrayal and doubt of His closest friends, He suffered the great indignity which the most innocent of us suffer when we are judged unjustly! He saw the pain in His mother's eyes and had to see His dream for the world turn into a horrible nightmare of rejection of His gospel, His ways and His very self!

• Even after His death, the soldiers' leader pierced His heart with a lance. It seems they couldn't rip Him apart any more than they possibly had done. He was beaten, pierced, and rejected even in death!

I cannot believe that anyone who has the slightest amount of faith could ever be disrespectful about a crucifix. When one stops to realize that God, Victim and Priest, died – in His human nature – on a cross the way Christ Jesus died, one must ask, why? The answer is so totally "mind blowing," because He loved us! Clearly, He could have asked His Father for 12 legions of angels (6,000 in a Roman legion x 12 legions = 72,000 angels!) to help Him and His Father would have granted His request! Furthermore, He said no one took His life from Him, He laid it down of His own accord when He so willed. What is He saying? Simply, that He went through all of this in order to open for us, for you and for me, the gates of heaven! He was not only the bridge between heaven and earth, He was (and is) heaven itself! In Jesus, heaven came to earth so that earth could be transformed into heaven! Jesus Christ suffered as the eternal Victim for all sin and, as the Great High Priest, He offered Himself, together with our own poor efforts at ridding ourselves of sin, to the Eternal God so that we might experience the Godhead in the most excellent way possible, that is, through God's own human nature, through His body and soul found within the Son.

To pause long enough so as to consider, to ponder all of the above, may take a little effort but it will make a world of difference in how I see myself, in what will, in the future, make me happy and, in the end, make the only real difference in me and in my life; a "difference" that may make an "eternal difference"! In the end, it is not in what I achieve, during my life, that matters; it is whether, when my life is over, and my days are gone, do I simply die, or do I die in the Lord? There is an "eternity" of difference between the two!

Amen!

THE UNSPOKEN – THE HIDDEN

They stood there on Calvary's slope: Those who loved the three hanging on the cross; those who were apathetic to them; the curious who enjoyed seeing the spectacular; those others who hated the victims and finally the traveling passersby! The day was windy, damp and generally unpleasant.

Every eye was on the executioners who stood ready, hammers and spikes in hand, to nail Him to the cross. Two soldiers held Him down, one knelt on His body, the other – with all his strength – pressed His right arm to the horizontal beam. The one executioner felt for the small opening in the wrist and with great gusto, took a spike and hammered it into the wood through the wrist of Jesus. The pain was excruciating! The second executioner did the same with the left arm. This done, they – all four of them – hoisted the horizontal beam into place on the vertical beam. One soldier tied His body to the cross, making sure the legs were fastened so the executioners could nail His feet to the plank sticking out from the lower part of the vertical beam. The centurion in charge, fastened Pilate's inscription of the charge which "merited" the event: Jesus of Nazareth, King of the Jews!

Mary lovingly looked into His face through His blood-matted hair. The voice which carried God's Divine Word was silent. She had to remember the moment that Gabriel asked her to become His mother. Now, here she asked herself if she should ever have said, "yes"? She recalled His birth and how sweetly the angels sang over Bethlehem's fields: what great hopes she had, what wonderful dreams. But wait! She couldn't have known; she simply could not have put it all together! He really had to go through all of this, she thought in disbelief? What did He ever do that was so terrible so as to merit this torture and death? She thought of her dear Joseph – if only he were here now, maybe he could have said something, he had such a way with words; maybe, he could have saved the boy he loved to call, "my Son"! She pondered, this Mother of Sorrows! She thought about what a good Son He had been, so thoughtful, loving, loyal and kind. She was so proud, so very proud of Him! Even during the past three years, He always kept her close to Himself. Since Joseph died, it was only the two of them! He made sure she had food and clean clothing to wear and comfortable bedding upon which to sleep and blankets to keep her warm. He seemed never to think about His own needs, He cared only for others.

Thought after thought, bombarded her mind! It had been pouring rain, her clothes were dripping wet and she hadn't even noticed! A strong hand and arm held her tightly. She was exhausted, tired and ever so weak. She thought: "But for John's arm holding me, I would fall onto the ground." "It will be okay dear Mother," the beloved disciple said. "He'll be okay. Something will happen to make it all go away." "John is so kind," she thought and "Jesus loved him so! But where is Simon and Andrew, James and all the others, where are they?" Confusion, that terrible cloud of senseless gray, covered her consciousness. She was so weak. She hadn't eaten for days. Her mouth was as dry as her body was wet from the rain. It was cold, so very, very cold.

She felt the warmth of two tiny hands holding her hand. They were constantly moving trying to get the blood to circulate so that feeling could be restored. Mary thought, "Magdalene, such a good, loving and caring soul. How she loved You, my Son, how she loved You! Jesus." She cried aloud: "We're here, we're all here and we love You, Jesus.

We're not going to leave You! We're here and we love You, we love You, we love You, my Son!" Simultaneously, John and Magdalene cried, "Yes, Lord ... Yes, Jesus, we love You ... we're right here with Your Mother. She'll be fine; we're never going to leave You, Jesus ... we love You, we love her, we love You!"

His head moved, ever so slowly, from its hanging, hauntingly silent and still position. He was trying to say something, trying to speak: "Woman, Mother, there is (now) your son ... Son, there is (now) your mother." The three beneath the cross never thought they would ever hear His voice again. They strained, from where they were standing, to draw closer to Him but the guards prohibited it. Hearing His words, they quickly looked into each other's eyes and burst out crying. They could not be consoled! Hearts broken take a goodly amount of time to heal! Empathy is a powerful emotion. The three felt – each in his/her own way – His every pain. Riveted to Him, they quietly "cheered on" His belabored breathing and strong will to live. The gasps of breath were farther and farther apart and were more shallow than when they (the Roman soldiers) first nailed Him to the cross. At least, they thought, He didn't cry aloud for the prophet or for God as He had done earlier! He seemed "settled," if that word could ever be used to describe such agony. Suddenly, once again, out of the long wait, He cried, "I thirst."

The soldiers were talking, but the watchers were unable to hear them. Quickly, one of them, showing a bit of sympathy, soaked a sponge in some vinegar and stuck it to a branch raising it to His mouth. He said, slowly, with a last breath, "It is finished."

It was over. His body hung limp on the cross; His head, His chin hitting His chest. The rain was falling much heavier and the lightning seemed to be brighter, the thunder, louder than ever. Off in the distance, because the sky was so dark, a fire could be seen near the Temple! Later, it would be said that the great curtain in the Temple was torn from top to bottom.

Beneath the cross, His cross, the three stood, weeping quietly. It was over. But, wait. The centurion looked up into the Crucified's face! "I guess I had better be sure He's dead." Taking a soldier's spear, the centurion thrust it into the heart of the King of the Jews. Blood, mixed with water, rushed out. Yes, it really was over! Finally over.

Gently, they worked the spikes out of His wrists and His feet. Slowly, they let the body, His body, down from the cross. The rain was torrential and the thunder deafening! Barely able to hold her arms up for herself, she held Him, the gentle hold and grasp of a loving mother. She cried, "Pity me," as she gazed up into the rain pouring down.

They slowly took Him from her and ever so gently, they brought Him into a tomb located nearby so that He could be washed, cleaned, dressed for burial. All having been done, she kissed His forehead and lips, told Him she loved Him and quietly walked away. Sealing the tomb, the broken mother, and grieving friends left as the long wait began!

Amen!

CONTEMPLATION – PRAYER

He had her eyes, her smile, her personality; no one could ever, knowing her, not call this Jesus from Nazareth, the son of Mary! They were always together. She walked behind the young donkey on which He rode as thousands came forward to welcome Him into Jerusalem. She smiled and laughed for joy as palm branches and cloaks were laid along His path. She was happy, so very, very happy. He, her Son, had, at last, been recognized for who He was! They really were listening, this crowd of people. They saw His goodness and experienced His love. How proud she was, little Mary of Nazareth, so young a mother, so recently a widow; her life would be joyful, despite her loss of dear Joseph. Look at Peter, look at James and John, why even Judas looked pleasant for a change! Things were going to be just fine. Here, in Jerusalem, things were going to be fine!

A few short days and what a difference to see. Beaten, broken, silent, humiliated and ripped from her heart, the Son she loved would be hauled away and thrown before the very people who hated Him most. Joy would give way to intense sorrow – as cries of "Hosanna" would yield to shouts of crucify Him, crucify Him!

Alone, frightened and confused, the mother expected to be arrested with her Son. She wanted to be with Him no matter where He was. She and He were always together. Even in a stable or along a road or in an open field, wherever He was, there was her home; wherever He was, there and only there was where she wanted to be.

His disciples had all left Him. Only John and Magdalene and a few of the women remained. "Where had they all gone? Were they arrested as well? Were they still alive?" She feared for them. It never crossed her mind that they deserted Him. She worried about them, it never entered her consciousness that they cared nothing about her. Like her Jesus, the little Mother cared only about others. She simply loved everyone. She never had bad thoughts about people, even when her better judgment suggested otherwise.

Outside of the courtyard of the high priest, she waited. Over there, next to the fire, it looked like Peter! "Simon," she cried aloud, "Simon, is that you?" Magdalene, always quite "savvy" stepped in front of the Mother of the Lord, deliberately blocking her view. "Dearest, Mother, that can't be Simon! Sit down on this rock, let us wait for Him, our Jesus, perhaps they will release Him soon ... let me put some blankets on the rock so you will be comfortable. Let us pray to God that Jesus and all the others will be safe."

As she spoke, the gates opened wide and the guards escorted Jesus through the path between the warming fires. The sad procession stopped suddenly as the Master turned in the direction of the man who resembled Simon. It was Magdalene who saw the man cover his face with his right arm as he practically fell into the fire. Bolting forward, he ran past the Master and the procession continued.

The mother couldn't see due to the height of the crowds. "Magdalene," she cried, "Did you see Jesus? Did you see my Son?" "Yes, little Mother, and He looks fine!" "O, thank God, thank God, I was so worried, so very, very worried," the little mother softly cried as she buried her head into John's loving chest.

Dearest Mother, your agony, your discipleship, your motherhood was challenged during that terrible week we call, holy. Soon, your Son would "pass over" from this world to the next. Soon, your heart would break, splinter and all but explode in pain! Still, the spirit within you, sustained by

God's Holy Spirit, would keep you together so that, for all of us, you might be an example of how we must act in crisis.

As you trusted the Father, so we must trust Jesus. As you "hung in there" despite the horrors that were happening, so we must "hang in there" until the long wait is over! A heart-beat from now, that wait will be over and we shall hear your voice and find God's Word. In heaven, we will at last be shown the meaning of why bad things do indeed happen to good people. In heaven, all the answers will be given and even make sense. We will never again have to feel sorry or sad because we're confused or angry. The divine answer to all life's confusion will take away whatever bitterness, hatred, alienation, rejection and despair we have ever experienced. Never again will rain darken or dampen the day of the picnic. The sun will always shine and the day will never die. Heaven will be lived in the heart of Jesus and that dark day which dawned on Calvary's hill, that day which sought to bury God will never again exist for the seed of God's love has flowered in God's garden, a place we call home, a place we call heaven!

Amen!

HIS WILL IN MY LIFE

1. *Using the images previously recorded, I shall stop every day to spend some quality time thinking about Jesus. I shall be there on Calvary with Mother Mary, Magdalene and John. I shall try to "feel" the terrible pain of that moment as the loves of my life suffer for love of me.*

2. *It was my sins which brought Jesus to His home. It was my sins which caused Mary's pain. Let me, like John and Magdalene be with Jesus and Mary in their hour of need as so often I invite them to be with me in my own hour of want!*

3. *Let me work at my salvation as if today were my last day on earth. Let me live today in the company of Jesus and Mary, for they are my destiny, my heaven, my best friends now and always.*

4. *Let me do something for them today as they did so very much for me each and every day of their lives on earth and as they continue to do now for me in heaven.*

Amen!

CHAPTER ELEVEN

THE MIRACLES OF JESUS CHRIST AND HOW I CAN MEDITATE ON THEM AND MAKE THEM COME ALIVE FOR ME – IS THIS REALLY POSSIBLE?

The wedding at Cana, where He turned water into wine; the cure of the sick man on the Sabbath; the multiplication of the loaves; and the walking on the sea; the restoration of sight to a blind man; the raising of Lazarus from death; these miracles are all recorded in John's gospel.

From Luke: the cure of a demoniac man and a leper; a paralyzed man cured along with the centurion's servant – all healed! The great exorcism of the Geraslene demoniac man and the multiplication of the loaves; the cure of the possessed boy and the 10 lepers, more and more miracles.

The Evangelist, Mark gives us the restoration of sight to Bartimaeus and the cure of a possessed boy; the healings of the blind man at Bethsaida; and the deaf mute of the Ten Cities. He fed 4,000 and healed the Cananite woman's daughter and walked on water!

Another time He fed 5,000 and healed the daughter of Jairus and the woman with a blood hemorrhage. He expelled the devils in Gerasa and calmed the storm at sea. Cures of a leper, the Capernaum paralytic and the man with a withered hand as well as Peter's mother-in-law and so many, many others! All miracles of Jesus Christ! At one point, when visiting Peter's home the "whole town" was brought to Him for healing!

Matthew tells of the restoration of sight He gave to the two blind men at Jericho and His feeding of the thousands by multiplying loaves and fishes. He heals suffering of all sorts: the Canannite women's daughter, and countless others, all healed, all restored to full health!

What really happened and why?

Jesus of Nazareth, the healer, the "bread king," in a real sense, began to "resent" people who flocked to Him to get "a quick fix" from physical, emotional, and psychological ills. Often, as time went on, Jesus would always heed the request of the person asking for a cure; however, He would tell them not to say anything to anyone about the healing. Rather, He would direct them to render a quiet prayer of thanks to God or perform some act of charity such as giving something to the Temple or showing themselves to the priests.

Traditional Christian teaching, almost as ancient as the Church itself speaks of four types of prayer: adoration, reparation, thanksgiving and petition. For most of us the fourth type of prayer gets, by far, the largest call! We are, as the English say, "a bidding (asking) people." Often, the prayers of the faithful at liturgy are called "bidding" prayers. We ask, we ask, and we ask some more!

In addition to being "bidding" people, we also "bid" or ask for anything we think we need to make our earthly lives more comfortable! Like the people of Jesus' time, we want what we want because we feel we simply can't live without it; we must have it and now! We've got to have it right now!

The prayer of petition is important; however, there are also prayers of adoration, reparation and thanksgiving. In addition, there are acts of divine worship, of incorporating God's holy will into my life! For example, as Catholics we "keep holy" the Lord's Day, Sunday, by attending Mass, by participating in the greatest act of reparation, adoration, thanksgiving and, yes, petition, we can make: to offer in an unbloody way, ourselves, with Jesus Christ, to the Eternal Father. How many of us fail to do this because we simply do not see (sometimes because we don't want to see) the relationship between our own wills and God's will!

If we believe that Jesus is Lord, our God, then we must accept His will for us. At the Last Supper, Jesus Christ clearly told us to do what we do at Mass on Sundays (and every day, save for Good Friday) to make Him present among us ("*Hoc facite in mean commemorationem*"). "Do this in memory of me" really means to "do this" (the imperative mood of the verb is used; this is the "mood" of command!) to make (Jesus) present among us! In a very real sense, we have no choice! This is how Jesus wants us to "keep holy" the Lord's Day. It is His will!

The question must then be posed: Does Jesus have other things He "wills" for us to do? Yes, this book and the bible and books about the Church and the bible are filled with God's will for us. We need to get to know God's will for us by reading and contemplating these works, pondering them as did Mary, the first and greatest disciple of her Son, Jesus Christ! Jesus Christ, we must remember is, for believers, the same as the Father (God). "Philip," Jesus replied, "after I have been with you all this time, you still do not know Me? Whoever has seen Me has seen the Father." (John 14:9). Jesus and the Father are one!

Returning to the point, we have developed a very dangerous "philosophy" of associating revealed truth (God's will for us) with how God judges us! We human beings today always want the "bottom line" on issues. We are not great readers of the classics but we love reading magazines (with lots of pictures) and newspapers. Better still, we are "audio nuts" and "visual freaks": we love listening to tapes or CDs or movies or TV. Whatever is easier is better! This whole "attitude" has invaded the way we teach and learn; but that is another argument for another book!

We have "bought religion" today much like we buy tapes, magazines, CDs, movies, etc., because we want to be entertained and, as a people with lots of time on our hands, have nothing better to do! Our "religion" is like an insurance policy: we never take it off the shelf unless we plan on using it! Usually, we never read the policy and hence do not even know what the policy says. We take it to a friend or an agent who can give us "the bottom line" (his or her interpretation of the policy) so we can know if indeed the policy is useful! Then back on the shelf goes the policy until need, felt need, takes over and off the shelf religious belief/practice comes!

Often, today, we hear of a shift in values having taken place. Youngsters in the first world today are indulged and introduced into the world of pleasures of all sorts! The thing to do today is to buy the latest products of pleasure and to be sure "our kids" have the latest and best of everything. It is also "necessary" for us to insure that the kids let other kids "see" the best and latest styles in clothing, toys and styles of life. Little more than a "fleeting glance" is necessary to realize what comes next! Gratification, self pleasure, un-controlled expectations, unrealistic demands on parents, grandparents and others creates the "me-first, pleasure sat-urated culture" which is totally unable to develop in the young people frustration-tolerance or anxiety-tolerance lev-els! The result is a society where people – mostly young pro-fessionals, men and women, now grown into adulthood – bump into one another, each talking on a cellular phone while trying to drive, walk down a street, or do other "worth-while" things. We must be readily available – or else! Beep-ers, cell phones, call-waiting, and countless other means of accessibility and connectedness rob our people of the nec-essary stress-deflecting and stress-suppressing agents and activities so necessary for real family bonding and unwind-ing!

Into the mix, we throw our relationship with Almighty God. We reduce Him and His Church to just another "stress creating moment" in a stress encumbered week! We find fault with this or that in the Church and, if we were really to be asked, we couldn't tell why! We resent our individual "time period designation" (allotted time allowed) for "Church" and we become upset and angry if the time goes over 45 to 59 minutes for Mass!

Stepping back, we can see what is happening: we are living in stress-related conditions and we are literally being controlled by the "attitudes" of a saturated, pleasure-first culture. Even our relaxation has taken on competitive forms (for example, golf). We are a people in false and vicious combat with horrible self-expectations and "win" philosophy, which rob us of our values, our relationships, our legitimate pleasures!

If there is one thing I have learned in over 23 years as the judicial vicar (chief judge) of a large archdiocesan marriage tribunal, it is that many relationships that end, are destroyed by the "savage kind of relationships" spouses have with each other. Materialism and self indulgence coupled with pride and exclusionary types of bonding result in the death of any relationship, most especially a marriage! Many couples will do anything to "avoid" having children until they are ready, "comfortable," so they say. Many relationships are never ready because the time frame is not expansive or wide enough to be inclusive of another person, like a child! We have become a society of "me first" people. We are exclusionary not inclusive; we are people who "must have" whatever we think we need (really, whatever we want) right here, right now and we never take "no!" for an answer!

We bring this attitude to our relationship with Jesus Christ and His Church, "our religion" (or so we call our "bonding" with Jesus). Once again, we can see we are doomed from the start. Jesus had nothing but "time, quality time" for us! He wanted, above all, to make us aware of our eternal home in heaven. He did all in His power to speak about heavenly things and priorities. With out current attitudes, we immediately "spurn" His agenda and throw our materialistic agendas into His face. Our "you had better give me a miracle or else" attitude simply doesn't "fly" with Jesus Christ.

John the Baptist resented people whose attitude was that a simple symbol like the water baptism he did for people was enough to rid them of sin or rather save their souls! The attitude has always been present in people except that today it's worse than ever. It's called the "easy way out is the best way."

If today we want a miracle from Our Lord there really are certain things we must do. Here they are. Please take time to ponder them:

1. We must have faith. We must live our faith. It must be real faith.

2. We must be inclusive people, loving, kind and charitable who enjoy giving more than taking or even more than getting. Mother Teresa of Calcutta was an example of this.

3. We must give Jesus quality, daily time at prayer and worship which is deeply flavored by acts and authentic sentiments of true devotion and genuine piety.

4. We must be concerned about the values Jesus Christ preached and we must genuinely want to live ourselves and teach others those values.

5. We must then examine the miracles Jesus performed and – where possible – imagine the motivation on the part of the person asking or the person whose good lifestyle spoke for them: (e.g., the elderly woman with the blood hemorrhage or the crippled man who had been waiting for decades for someone to put him into the pool for the angelic stirring of the waters).

6. Having prepared ourselves by prayer, true conversion of mind and heart, entirely opened to God's Almighty will

and Providence, and having asked the help of the Holy Spirit, Our Lady and the saints, we may request a miracle. The request should be placed entirely before the tribunal of the Blessed Trinity, made through the blood of Jesus, Our Lord, and opened to whatever be the outcome of God's holy will.

7. Finally, it is solely up to God as to whether or not the outcome of our preparation and our prayer might lead to a "miracle" or not. Most certainly, if we truly prepare ourselves and pray accordingly, we should know a great peace of mind and resignation of person. Our hearts too will be at peace. That, for most of us, constitutes "a miracle."

THE UNSPOKEN – THE HIDDEN

"Ask, and you will receive. Seek, and you will find. Knock, and it will be opened for you. For the one who asks, receives. The one who seeks, finds. The one who knocks, enters." (words of Jesus, Matt. 7:7-8).

Yes Lord, I ask, I seek, I knock but many times my preparation to receive, to discover, to enter is not enough. My faith is weak and my prayer of true adoration of Your Godhead, is simply flawed through my own fault!

I must remember that as a faith response "triggers" a response from You and lack of faith truly saddens and disappoints You to the point of Your being unable to perform many, if any miracles, so I must be filled with faith, good works, confidence and resignation to Your will if I hope to receive a favor!

I think of that woman who suffered for 12 years with a blood hemorrhage: "If only I can touch His cloak," she thought, "I shall get well." (Matt. 9:21). She did, He said. "Courage, daughter! Your faith has restored you to health." That very moment the woman got better. (Matt 9:22). On the other hand, there were many people who simply wanted to test Him and, to teach a lesson, He would cure them. A case in point is the man with a shriveled hand. Having questioned Him, and to test Him, after Jesus had answered them, the leaders of the people brought the poor man before Jesus. To Him the Lord replied: "Stretch out your hand." He did so, and it was perfectly restored; it became as sound as the other. (Matt. 12:9-13). Note that to one, He responded to her faith, her prayer and her suffering. To the other, to teach or clarify a lesson, He responded. What luck for the man with a shriveled hand!

We next see in the anguish of the Sidonian Canaanite woman, still another deep "other-conscious" loving concern which prompted a miracle. He tested her. A woman of lesser faith would have left in disgust. She asked Him to cure her daughter. He told her that His mission was to the lost in Israel and that: "It is not right to take the food of sons and daughters and throw it to the dogs." (Matt. 15:26). He was really testing her faith! She responded: "Please, Lord, ... even the dogs eat the leavings that fall from their masters' tables." (Matt. 15:27). He then observed: "Woman, you have great faith! Your wish will come to pass." The Scripture tells us that at that very moment, her daughter got better. (Matt. 15:28).

In each case it is to reward a living, committed faith and/or to teach a lesson that brings about a miracle!

In the mass healings which He performed, as in the feeding of the thousands, that which prompted the wondrous happening seemed to again be the needs of the people. Faith in Jesus seems to have called them together. Crowds of people, Scripture observes, were "greatly astonished" (cf. Matt. 15:31) at all the wonderful miracles being accomplished.

In the case of the man with the possessed boy, not even the disciples (the apostles) were able to cure him. In reply to this state of affairs, Jesus responded to His own disciples: "What an unbelieving and perverse lot you are! How long must I remain with you? How long can I endure you? Bring him (the possessed boy) here to Me!" (Matt.17:17-18). Jesus cured the boy by driving out the demon! Note the anger, justified anger, in the remarks of our Lord. Peppered with a bit of discouragement, Jesus' anger shows His justified response to His disciples whose lack of faith prohibits the requested miracle from taking place.

Here we see what happens to the faithless minister when his faith is so weak that he simply cannot call healing to take place. In this "cameo" from the life of Christ, we see how the Lord treats disciples who publicly profess one thing and live another! If we say we are Christ's disciples and have "less than a mustard seed of faith" are we truly His disciples? If we ask Him for a miracle, do we have the faith response that is absolutely required? Here, the person asking has the faith, the disciple/apostle doesn't, yet the healing does take place because of Christ's responding to the "little people" whose faith is true, justified, and complete.

"Blindness" is another real problem with true faith. There are many forms of blindness: some, such as physical loss of sight or vision; some, the direct result of a failure to hear, to ponder, to understand the ways of Jesus. James and John, the sons of Zebedee, are disciples of Christ. One day, their very "pushy" mother approached our Lord and boldly asked for the impossible. "Promise me that these sons of mine will sit, one at Your right hand and the other at Your left, in Your kingdom." (Matt. 20:21). She was formal, forward and direct in her approach. She may even have had faith. But, we ask, what kind of faith? Did she realize for what she was asking? Had she any idea of what/where His kingdom was? Clearly, something is missing in this "cameo" from the life of Jesus Christ.

Jesus answers Mrs. Zebedee as directly, as formally and as forwardly, as she requested the favor of Him: "You do not know what you are asking. Turning toward James and John, He asked "Can you drink of the cup I am to drink of?" "We can," they said. He told them, "From the cup I drink of (suffering), you shall drink. But sitting at My right hand or My left hand is not Mine to give. That is for those to whom it has been reserved by My Father." (Matt. 20:22-23).

Sometimes, we don't realize for what we ask. Sometimes, we ask for things we have no right to ask or expect to receive. Hence, in these situations, Jesus cannot respond positively to our requests.

One final comment on the James, John and Mother Zebedee "cameo:" the response/reaction of the other 10 apostles is interesting: On hearing this (remember I said Mrs. Zebedee was rather forward and loud), " ... the other 10 (apostles) became indignant at the two brothers." (Matt. 20:24). This resulted in Jesus Christ's teaching on the virtue of the true humble servant of God! Jesus spoke most sternly to the Twelve, including among the listeners, Mrs. Zebedee (and companion mothers) concluding: "Anyone among you who aspires to greatness must serve the rest, and whoever wants to rank first among you must serve the needs of all. Such is the case with the Son of Man who has come, not to be served by others, but to serve, to give His own life as a ransom for the many." (Matt. 20:26-28). The lesson is clear: be careful for what you ask ... you may get more than you at first expected!

Juxtaposed against this incident is the simple, wonderful and brave faith of the two blind men in Jericho. They cried to the Lord to pity them. Pity, what a powerful word! Yet, that correctly expresses their emotion, their real-felt need. "Lord, Son of David, have pity on us." (Matt. 20:30). Note, they asked as much for each of them as for both of them together. When the crowd began to scold them in an effort to bring them to silence, their bravery called them to cry the louder: "Lord, Son of David, have pity on us!" Jesus then stopped and (no doubt knowing full well their request) called out to them (ignoring the crowd), "What do you want Me to do for you?" "Lord," they told Him, "open our eyes!" Moved with compassion, Jesus touched their eyes, and im-

mediately they could see; and they became His followers."
(Matt. 20:30-34). Jesus responded to them both as individuals and as a group of two. James and John and the two formerly blind disciples can teach us much about what to request of the Lord; how to request it and the attending circumstances which "trigger" Christ's favorable responses.

James and John had been, by this time, around our Blessed Lord for some time; however, you would never know it. The two blind men hadn't even met Jesus and, from their response, you can see they really knew Him and followed Him immediately! This is the difference between real faith and empty faith. Whatever happened to the two formerly blind new disciples we never learn. Maybe in heaven we will learn that they are among the greatest disciples of Christ who taught victims of blind faith how to really see!

CONTEMPLATION – PRAYER

Lord Jesus Christ, as I walk in Your footprints, I too meet all kinds of people. Some are friends, most don't know me, some may be irritated by my presence: what I look like, what I talk like, my position in life, etc., some may even hate me; yet, all should know that I am Your disciple, Your follower, Your friend by how I speak, walk, think and act! Help me to be an engaging disciple. Help me to hear the cries of the people whose paths cross my path. Help me to understand that, like me, they are looking for miracles to make happen in their lives less pain, emptiness and loneliness. Help me to be a true viaduct of Your healing, miraculous love.

Lord, as You have shown compassion to the broken, let me show compassion as well. If it is within my power to bring relief to the pain of others from emptiness, loneliness or depression, enable me Lord to so do! Let me not think of myself, of my own position in Your family; rather, let me think only of Your love, Your care, Your compassion for all of us redeemed by Your precious blood. That blood spilled for us on Calvary! Let me see behind the anger and resentment of the abject poor, the call of the Father to each of us to practice justice based on love. Let me realize that by means of authentic discipleship You are here in my life to bring me into Your heavenly life!

Let me understand that I may very well pass these poor people along heaven's streets and they might wonder why I, claiming to be a disciple of Jesus, never reached into my pocket to help them! They might wonder why I couldn't spend some few minutes to listen or to give some change to them because I couldn't "inconvenience" myself when, Lord, all You did for me, O God, was to totally inconvenience Your-self!

Help me, dear Lord, not to ask favors for myself that I really don't need! Sometimes, the only "Jesus" the poor, elderly in convalescent homes, the "throw-aways" of life know are people like me who claim to be Your apostles, Your disciples.

Around our necks, dear Lord, we wear crucifixes, crosses, medals of Our Lady or the saints. We wear these symbols and other signs of commitment to You, to show the world that we believe in You. How then can we fail to look at You, to see You, in the broken of our world who have a far more justifiable call on Your healing than do we? We are the hands You sent to heal, the voices You sent to comfort, the money You sent to relieve the ravages of poverty in all of its forms! We are living extensions of Your miracles to our brothers and sisters and our parents.

When we see the loneliness, emptiness and pain of the elderly awaiting the final call to enter eternal life, do we take the time to hear life's wisdom locked into a weak voice or dimmed eyes? Do we see the beauty in these priceless human beings? So many are locked away in institutions because their families will not care for them; not because they cannot care for them, but because it is too inconvenient to their wealthy lifestyles to care for them! How You must judge these, Lord!

We remember poor Lazarus, the beggar, who had nothing here on earth and the rich man who had everything! Death, that great judge, reversed their positions in heaven! It was Your own Father whose justice demanded that painful, horrible consequence to the rich man's decision not to provide for the poor Lazaruses of the world. (read: Luke 16:19-31). He went directly to hell-fire and Lazarus went directly into You, dear God. Let this never happen to me.

Let me do good while I am able and never count the cost to my pocketbook, to my lifestyle or to my calendar! Let me remember that it is not in how I invest my money or in how much money I have to invest as I live; it is, rather, in how I live and in what I do to reflect Your love, Your concerns, Your values that truly will determine what treasures await me hereafter. Let me never, Lord, worry about the tomorrows of life at the cost of today's Christ-like challenges You send to me.

Let me take care of today's opportunities to live as Christ and all the tomorrows and eternity itself will be taken care of by the Father who sees, loves and rewards, what is done in the secret places of my heart.

Amen!

His will in my life

1. I will strive to be Christ-centered, Christ-directed, Christ-focused, Christ-celebrating in all the events of my life.

2. When asking for a miracle, I will first ask myself: is that for which I am asking "window-dressing," "frosting on the cake" or something that will really help me to seek the kingdom of God and to be a better disciple of Christ, Jesus?

3. I will see Christ in others, especially the poor, the un-born, the elderly in my society. I will give them some of my time each and every day. I will help to improve their God-giv-en dignity by contributing some of my wealth to charity in the hopes that God will not judge me too harshly on my own day of judgment.

4. I pray that God will give me the greatest miracle of all: To save my own immortal soul by helping to save others' souls. "Lord Jesus, help me to always remember that I am but a heart-beat away from Your judgment and help me to live ac-cordingly. Let me never be pride-filled or arrogant but help me to be a loving servant to all. Let me remember that today the only real authority and power is to walk humbly with my Master, my Lord, as You walked so humbly in our footsteps, Lord, Second Person of the Blessed Trinity, our God, our hope, our final destiny in heaven."

Amen!

CHAPTER TWELVE

*THE FRIENDS OF JESUS: HIS DISCIPLES
AND HIS APOSTLES
WERE HIS CONSTANT COMPANIONS.
WHAT CAN THEY TEACH US ABOUT JESUS?*

Mark in Chapter 6, and Luke in Chapter 9, give us the Mission of the Twelve Apostles:

Mark's Narrative

"Jesus summoned the Twelve and began to send them out two by two, giving them authority over unclean spirits. He instructed them to take nothing on their journey but a walking stick – no food, no traveling bag, not a coin in the purses in their belts. They were, however, to wear sandals. 'Do not bring a second tunic!' He said, and added: 'Whatever house you find yourself in, stay there until you leave the locality. If any place will not receive you or hear you, shake its dust from your feet in testimony against them as you leave.' With that they went off, preaching the need of repentance. They expelled many demons, anointed the sick with oil, and worked many cures."
- Mark 6:7-13.

Luke's Narrative

"Jesus now called the Twelve together and gave them power and authority to overcome all demons and to cure disease. He sent them forth to proclaim the reign of God and heal the afflicted. Jesus advised them: 'Take nothing for the journey, neither walking staff nor traveling bag; no bread, no money. No one is to have two coats. Stay at whatever house you enter and proceed from there. When people will not receive you, leave that town and shake its dust from your feet as a testimony against them.' So they set out and went from village to village, spreading the good news everywhere and curing diseases."
- Luke 9:1-6.

Luke 10:1-16 sees the Lord having appointed 70 others and sent them on ahead of Himself to do essentially the same mission as He had given the Twelve. All are to carry the message of warning that the kingdom of God is at hand. Clearly, the Twelve and the others are happy, as when they return to Jesus they report all to have gone well.

In Matthew 16:24-28, in Mark 8:34-9:1 and in Luke 9:3-27, we see spelled out for us the conditions of and for being a true disciple of Jesus Christ. These conditions are:
- self-denial
- taking up (carrying) one's own cross
- being able to "lose one's life" for Christ's sake
- this must be done at all costs on risk of one's salvation ...

The call of "the Twelve" appears in Matthew 10:1-4; Mark 3:13-19 and Luke 6:12-16. All three evangelists list the Twelve as: Simon Peter; his brother, Andrew; James son of Zebedee; John, son of Zebedee; Philip and Bartholomew; Thomas and Matthew the tax collector; Thaddaeus; Simon, the Cananaean; James son of Alphaeus; and Judas Iscariot who betrayed the Lord.

When one has listed the names of the Twelve, their mission (work) and the cautions the Lord attaches to their mission and their persons, one gets a picture of an enormous job with eternal, god-like requirements based on the conviction that Jesus Christ is truly God whose kingdom is in heaven. If you accept these truths of faith, all else falls into place. If you doubt, or don't, everything falls apart.

The Twelve and the 70 were the constant companions of Christ. How else could they have learned enough from Him to preach and to proclaim His gospel? He had to trust them before sending them forth. He had to train them in what exactly was to be their jobs as His ambassadors. These men knew Jesus Christ. They knew Him well. They fully accepted Him or they would never have taken the risks they took for Him and for His gospel.

What can they, the Twelve and the 70, teach us about Jesus Christ? Jesus had told them that their love and commitment had to be total! He said some "impossible" things, made some all-embracing demands of His disciples. "He who loves father or mother more than Me is not worthy of Me; and he who loves son or daughter more than Me is not worthy of Me, and he who does not take his cross and follow Me is not worthy of Me." (Matt. 10:37-39). Luke quotes Jesus: "If any one comes to Me and does not hate his own father and mother and wife and children and brothers and sisters, yes, and even his own life, he cannot be My disciple. Whoever does not bear his own cross and come after Me, cannot be My disciple." (Luke 14:26-27).

For a man to attempt, under these conditions, to follow Jesus, is similar today to spending a lifetime joining and going through "boot camp" after "boot camp," day after day, of groups like the U.S. Marine Corps, Annapolis' Naval Academy and West Point's Army Academy! I once heard of a person who joined a local police force and after having gone through their training academy, she then joined another police department (a much larger department in another state) and went through the department's training academy; she then joined a state police department and went through that police academy; finally, she joined a federal law enforcement agency and went through that training academy. I heard recently that the person was full of nervous twitches and blinks! We human beings are not all called to be Rambo!

Is Jesus Christ making unreasonable demands on His disciples? Can we really follow Him; are we capable of following Him under these conditions?

Realistically, I believe one of the greatest proofs of Christ's Divine Mission is found in the response to the question: Is one capable of following Jesus Christ given the demands He sets down for His disciples, His followers? The answer is both "yes" and "no." "Yes" if one puts one's entire faith in Jesus and lives for Him, confident that He will take care of the things in our lives. Countless numbers of people have done this. They have placed all their burdens in life aside and taken on the burden of gospel proclamation. Not only clergy and religious have responded in this way; laity, in greater and greater numbers are finding ways and means of total lifestyle changes in order to accept the challenges of a Carpenter from Nazareth who lived nearly 2,000 years ago!

Like people who have accepted the mission of Christ down through the ages, many people today give themselves totally to the Lord. People with families, for example, leave the comforts of the United States to become Maryknoll associates, workers for the gospel, in poor third world countries. Mothers and fathers literally choose to raise their children with the abject poor of the world because Christ has been lifted from the ages and become incarnate in the poor of the world.

Something inside of us seems to drive us to do the "impossible" because we believe that much in the "incredible," i.e., that God became flesh in Jesus Christ is true and that real life and true living begins after death. That what we do here and now will truly determine what we will be like in eternity. We run the race so as to win the crown. It doesn't make any sense from a purely human perspective, but it makes perfect sense from the divine point of view.

The truly committed (to Christ) of today are every bit like the disciples of 2,000 years ago. They are one and the same! They see Jesus and the job He gives them today as

worth it. True, it (the Christ given call to discipleship) con-
tradicts the philosophies of materialism, extreme capital-
ism, socialism and communism. It is directly opposed to the
pleasure principle of how many people live their lives today.

What has been said of the philosophy of exclusion, that
which drives the world of advertising today, is and stands in
direct opposition to the way of Jesus and His faithfilled disciples. Jesus is inclusive. His very essence (the Second Person of the Blessed Trinity), is, in terms of relating to
humanity, redeeming! He redeems us from our sins; He redeems us from evil! To redeem us He must relate to us. He
must relate to us in such a way and in such a manner as to
take us from where we were (or are) to where He wants us
to be. He must get inside of us as well as outside of us. He
must be closer to us than is the air in our lungs or the blood
in our arteries! He is the Redeemer. He is the primary mover
in the act of redemption! He shows us the way and gives us
the "how to" get there! He presents the program and asks us
whether or not we want to join or participate. The choice is
ours. He gives us help in making the decision to follow Him.
This help is called grace. He provides opportunities to interact with fellow pilgrims like ourselves who help and assist
us on our journey. But ... the journey is spiritual. The journey is supernatural. Apart from the spiritual/supernatural-
ly revealed aspects, the "redemption" and the Redeemer
Himself, makes no sense whatsoever!

The disciples of Jesus believed. Because they believed
in Jesus, they performed the works He gave them to do!
They practiced the spiritual and corporal works of mercy,
they observed the authority structure He established and
followed the challenge of evangelizing the world. As motivation and as a reward, they believed they would live with God
forever in paradise. Fully aware that the "goods" of this

world were transitory, the disciples "put all their eggs in one basket." Like St. Francis of Assisi, they made their lives like that of Jesus Christ. Like Mother Teresa of Calcutta, they modeled their lives on the life of Jesus.

For the true and faithful disciple, heaven is not something awaiting somewhere out there in space. Heaven is here and now! Heaven is having Christ living within, through Word and Sacrament. Heaven is the peace which is impossible for the world to have or to give. Heaven is a freedom which is never license (i.e., doing whatever I feel like despite the rules). Heaven begins here and now and is fully lived and celebrated after death in eternity. Heaven is what Jesus Christ, His Blessed Mother, the blessed in heaven, is all about. Heaven is, as has been said, a heart-beat away. Heaven is, above all, being a constant companion with Jesus who, living within us, teaches us everything we need to know now, tomorrow and forever.

Amen!

THE UNSPOKEN – THE HIDDEN

Peter, denied; Thomas, doubted; Judas, betrayed You, Lord Jesus Christ. James and John Zebedee were proud and boastful and didn't care about how anyone felt. Saul of Tarsus became Paul the apostle and then began a lifetime journey of purification from his egotism and his pride. Philip was faithless and wanted to see the face of the Father; he never understood the meaning of what You had said during Your public ministry. The three closest to you, Peter, James and John, slept when You told them to watch and pray. They had to have their own way. They all had to have their own way.

Often, so many of Your disciples lost interest in You and Your ways because their agendas were all that really mattered to them. Like so many of us today, our agendas (stated agendas and hidden agendas) are really all that truly matters. We use each other as "sounding boards" to "field" our ideas to ourselves and to others. We are simply not good listeners. We don't hear each other because we're usually thinking of the next thought and how we are going to formulate it or how we are going to present it. We're very much like radios: one way transmission!

Your disciples knew that You would ask for an accounting of the responsibilities You had given them. They fully understood Your parables, especially those dealing with their own accountability. Many invested their talents and gained new talents, like the two blind beggars to whom You restored sight. They became Your disciples, they followed You.

What did the crowds who followed You really talk about? How did they speak to one another? Did You overhear what was said by Your disciples as they traveled the roads with You for three years? Did Your mother speak with You of their many concerns? Was there ever, dear Lord, an opportunity to debrief? Did anyone ever stop to listen and to hear all that You said? Did they understand Your disappointment with Your disciples who would not believe in Your Eucharist? So many let You think Your words were understood! One hears Your resounding disappointment in Your discourse on the Bread of Life (cf. John 6:25-65). You challenged them to accept You and the way You wanted to reach down through the ages to people everywhere and in all places. The Holy Eucharist was the means You instituted to literally "get inside" of people so that for all time You could change the hearts of all people, everywhere and always!

Who would ever have thought that Emmanuel would be not only "God with us" but, by means of the Blessed Sacrament, "God within us"?

For our part, we always want to do "our thing." We always want to do what we want. We are a people lost in ourselves! We are totally unworthy of You and Your love. We are not a lovable people. Either as individuals or as a people, we always "come up" looking toward what is "in it" for ourselves and not what is best for You, dearest Lord Jesus.

Yet, we want everything but we don't want to pay the price. There is an old saying: a cynic knows the price of everything and the value of nothing! We are "super selfish" cynics! We all believe that everyone has an angle, everyone is solely out for himself or herself.

Thomas, Your apostle, would not believe in You until he saw You; until he put his fist into Your side and his fingers into the wounds in Your feet and wrists. How foolish! When I think of how vividly the image is, it amazes me that when You did see Thomas You did not become so angry with him, because of his arrogance, that You continued to let him live! Lord, all You did was to forgive him. You accepted his silly act of "belief" – but it wasn't belief! Belief takes place when, without seeing, we act. Thomas refused to believe! Finally, You appeared and Thomas saw. He really didn't have "to believe." Lord, You gave him knowledge! He literally saw You and physically felt You. He heard You and responded to You.

So many of us today want to see You, to feel You, to hear You! In our arrogance, we demand a manifestation of Your divine Person. We even convince ourselves that, should we be so favored, we would change our lives. The reality is just the opposite! In the story of the rich man and the beggar Lazarus, You told us how God reacts to requests following death and judgment. When we die, we bring with us only our good deeds that our virtues, to speak for us. The rich man's conduct, his failure to help poor Lazarus and do the other good deeds that he should have done, merited an eternity in hell! When he asked for personal relief, You, in Your justice, would not permit it. When he asked You to send Lazarus who rested within You, to the rich man's brother in order to warn them about this, You again, in justice, refused this favor.

Lord, let me do always what You expect of me. Let me go beyond what is expected of me and do always what You "dream" ideally I should do to please You. Let me be much better than what is expected; Lord, let me become a saint! Help me to choose those paths in life traveled by Your faithful apostles and disciples. Help me to live my life as if I would die today and help me to work at my salvation as if I would live forever!

Lord, from Your apostles, I have seen the true call of authentic conversion based on true humility. Only when each had given his all and emptied himself out of his own egotism and selfishness did he truly begin to resemble You!

You were always present and available to Your apostles and disciples. You answered their questions, no matter how much they showed they hadn't listened to Your teachings. You gave them all the time they demanded and never questioned them if they showed the slightest sincerity. Dear Lord, help me to treat all others in my life as You treated Your friends, Your disciples. Then, dear Lord, when I do at last die, I will die in You, the Lord, and You will welcome me home, Your home, heaven, now my home with You, forever.

Amen!

CONTEMPLATION – PRAYER

Lord, I have tried to follow You as did Your apostles and disciples; however, like Simon, I am often filled with myself: boastful and proud; like Saul, I am arrogant and self-righteous; like Thomas, doubt fills my mind; like Philip, I demand too much; and like James and John Zebedee, I am far too conceited. Lord, You worked with them; yes, Lord, You worked Your transforming, transfiguring love within these men and so many, many others. Lord, with You and because of You, they changed!

Teach me not to give up on You or on myself! Give me the prayerful spirit of Mary of Bethany, Lazarus' sister, coupled with the work-ethic of Martha, her sister. Let me have the best possible relationship with You. Like Lazarus of Bethany, Your closest friend, let me provide the respite from cares, the kind of cares which come from so many hours of work in the vineyard of teaching and proclaiming the gospel. Like Magdalene, let me truly repent of my sins and fall deeply in love with You. Like faithful John, Your trusted disciple, let me put You first in my life. Like good Nicodemus, let me be guileless, let me reflect Your goodness in my ways of life.

Lord, Your good companions with whom You walked this earth really loved You! Yes, many made mistakes, serious mistakes; but all of them corrected their mistakes and their ways save for Judas. Like Simon who became the Rock, let me accept suffering in order to win souls to Your way of life. Like Paul, let me be motivated to work relentlessly for the gospel, spreading the faith everywhere. Like Thomas, help me to accept all peoples and give my life in service to the evangelization of all peoples! Like the saints of the early church, the Middle Ages and the saints of today, help me to identify Your footprints in the many footprints along life's shore. Help me, once I locate them, to carefully identify my own life's crosses and to carry them as I walk within Your footprints. Only then, dear Lord, can I truly be a faithfilled, faithful disciple whose mind, heart and body resembles Yours, dear Jesus.

Let me not give in to human respect, arrogance or pride in any of its manifestations. Lord, we are all victims of sin, of our sinful inclinations. We are tempted to cheat and steal at the price of another's treasure. Judas Iscariot You called to be an apostle. You did not call him to be a traitor. You called him to become a saint! Early on, dear Lord, he betrayed You. He stole from the common purse. He stole because he wanted money he had no right to have.

Lord, I doubt that You would ever have denied Judas Iscariot anything! He was just as much a "called apostle" as were any of the other eleven! What made him different from them was his attitude and his continuing sin! He never repented! He never owned-up to his sin! He never identified his sin. Driven to greater and greater selfishness, he finally "celebrated" his sin, the betrayal of the Son of God, by "selling" You for 30 pieces of silver! Lord, in Judas we see something of ourselves each and every time we steal another's good name or reputation.

Our judgment of neighbor is always clouded by our own motivations and prejudices. We are not qualified to judge, dear Lord, and You have warned us that as we judge others so You will judge each of us! Lord, help us to learn forgiveness from You. Not only did You forgive Your disciples' betrayal, denial, doubt, and cowardice, you also restored those who honestly and sincerely sought to ask for Your forgiveness and to be restored to Your love.

Lord, help me to help others as they too struggle with the real priorities of eternal life. Let me never compromise my own priorities as I continue my pilgrimage journey to heaven. Let me continue to learn from today's disciples and apostles how to welcome You, O King of the ages, into my life, my world, my heart of hearts in the here and now and forever hereafter.

Amen!

HIS WILL IN MY LIFE

1. I resolve to learn from the good example of others how to be a faithful disciple of Jesus Christ.

2. I resolve today to examine my own conscience and to live and work at improving my choices based on what Jesus would have me do.

3. I resolve to support the vocations to priesthood, diaconate, religious life, marriage and family life and committed single lifestyles.

4. I promise to pray daily for candidates to Church related ministries, the Christ disciples of today. I will support them in all the activities of their ministry.

5. Finally, I shall try to give good examples and encourage all in the ways of genuine Christian discipleship. Help me, Lord Jesus.

CHAPTER THIRTEEN

HOW DOES JESUS CHRIST DEAL WITH EVIL?
WHAT ARE THE THINGS THAT MADE JESUS
CHRIST UNHAPPY AND REACT?
HOW CAN I DO ALL I CAN TO BE PEACEFUL
AND BE READY,
A HEARTBEAT AWAY FROM NOW,
TO ENTER HEAVEN?

This chapter will be different. It is divided into two sections: the first is the upper half of the chapter's title; the second half are prayers which I composed and which I sincerely hope will bring peace to the reader.

Evil comes from the Evil One. We call him the Devil, Satan, the Fallen Angel, the Diabolical Prince, Lucifer. He was not created a devil, the source of evil. He made himself that source by challenging Almighty God. We never win when we challenge the Creator. We always lose! The Old Testament is filled with people whose choices challenged Almighty God and lost the battle and the war.

Scripture reminds us in the Ten Commandments, in the very first commandment, that God is truly a "jealous" God who calls us to singular fidelity. "Hear, O Israel, the Lord is God alone and I shall have no strange gods before me (by your choices)!" We all choose what we do each and every time we decide on living life to the fullest. We decide on who will be our friends (and who will be our enemies); we decide on how close (or how distant) will be our associations with people, places and things in life. We decide not to decide and that as well is a choice. When we fail to change our sinful habits, we choose to keep them; when we say we're going to quit smoking or quit drinking alcohol and deliberately continue to buy cigarettes or alcohol, we have chosen to continue our habits despite our resolutions to the contrary.

Sins of omission are equally evil as are sins of commission! All involve choices, choices to do or not to do good are, by deliberate act or non-action, decisions for evil! Apathy, for example, is truly evil!

Earlier, I mentioned the necessity of challenging ourselves and others in gospel values. To challenge someone to be a good disciple is essential if we are to do the work of an evangelist. The life of St. Paul is a clear witness to this. Paul ran the race so as to win the crown. What crown? The crown of a true apostle, a good disciple.

Jesus had absolutely no room for apathy, indifference or lukewarmness in His life or the lives of His disciples. He spoke of what would happen if this type of conduct came before Him in judgment. He said He would "vomit" this out of His mouth! Did He mean just the actions (or non-actions) of His disciples or, rather, did He mean the disciples themselves? I think a close look at the text sees Him throwing away the disciple who tried to corrupt the gospel!

Evil's many manifestations prop-up everywhere! We are in the day and age of explaining things away. Even our "*raison d'etre*" for being Christians can be explained away by saying we are as we are and God will not condemn us for needing to feel good about ourselves! Yes, we need to feel good about ourselves. We need to accept ourselves, yes, but NOT as we are! We are called to change our lives, our witness into accurate reflections of our living Lord; living within us and within our brothers and sisters in the faith!

When Jesus drove the money changers out of the Temple, He did so because they were turning God's house into a den of thieves! (cf. John 2:13-25). I find it interesting to note the final passage in John 2:24, 25. "For His part, Jesus would not trust Himself to them because He knew them all. He needed no one to give Him testimony about human nature. He was well aware of what was in man's heart." Yes, to be aware of "what was in man's heart," is truly a gift from God! Jesus knew sin just as well as He knew what human nature was all about. Man is capable of reaching the heights of holiness; he is also free to choose evil and free not to choose the desired good!

Jesus is hurt, disappointed by a lack of faith, a lack of

proper response to His call to holiness. He sees all holiness as coming from His relationship with the Church He wishes to establish. He is the essence, the Source of Divine Love. All that is truly good and holy in the Church emanates from that love Source! Like the wheel pictured below, Jesus, the source of Divine Love, gives us everything we need to win

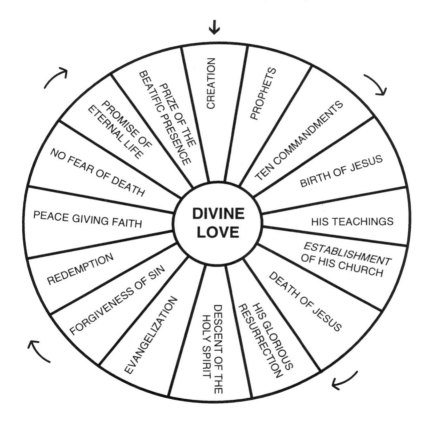

our supernatural birthright.

Evil inhibits the flow of Divine love in the human condition. It blocks (or attempts to block) this flow of love. Objective evil is divided, as has been noted, into two divisions: directly committed acts of evil and directly omitted actions of good. When we do the "committed actions" or "fail to do the required good actions" we are in serious danger of sin. Sin takes place when we deliberately choose the evil over the good and when we fail to do the good commanded by God of us. In this action (or lack of action), we become involved in the world of evil. Evil is a true distortion of the "final cause," i.e., the reason why we were made. It seeks the desired "good" in the here and now. It seeks always to pleasure the self even at the cost of one's eternal salvation.

The reactions of Jesus to committed chosen acts of evil is always immediate, swift and highly emotional. He simply cannot abide evil! He sees evil as a deliberate affront to all He is. He sees evil as the opposite of His Father's will. Recall that even in the Garden of Gethsemani (the Mount of Olives), he prayed to the heavenly Father to remove the cup of suffering from which He was about to drink; yet, He stated immediately, " ... Your will (Father) be done." (Matt. 26: 42). He submitted His all to the Father's eternal will. He simply could never accept any other course of action. God's holy will had to be done. "Thy will be done on earth as it is (done) in heaven." He became unhappy and reacted whenever the will of the Father was questioned. He became totally outraged by acts of hypocrisy, of pretending to do one thing and actually doing another. He cautioned us about not performing our good deeds for others to see. He reminds us that when we do such things and people see us, we have had our reward!

I'm sure that all of us continue to give of our time, talent and treasure – in part at least – so that others will see us and think the better of us. This choice certainly displeases the Lord, who seeks to purify our hearts.

Simply put, the entire gospel of Jesus Christ is about a love affair that God, in Jesus, wants to have with each of us individually and all of us as His people! He has no time for second best! He wants us to love Him and live our lives for Him. Short of this, He has no time for our weaknesses. His love, His life is given to the greater honor and glory of the Blessed Trinity and for the redemption of the world from the bonds of evil and sin. He wants us ideally, to the best of our ability, to live and love as He gave us an example. He spent His life trying to teach us how to live. He will tolerate our weaknesses if we try to correct them. He will read our minds and our hearts before He judges our deeds.

Trying to be better people by making use of God's graces to overcome our weaknesses is all Jesus asks of us. Our resolution each day is to be the best I can be today; that is all He wants. To do this is to TRUST JESUS; not to do this is the direct path leading to self-destruction. We are His faithfilled people called to be faithful, called first, last, and always to TRUST JESUS and live here and hereafter in heaven.

Amen!

INTENT

I can really do all in my power to be peaceful and to be ready, a heartbeat from now, to enter heaven by living the call to be holy. For the Catholic, that call is found in Scripture and in the teachings of the holy Roman Catholic Church. That call to be holy has been the sole topic and direction of this little text, a short course in devotion, that bridge between prayer and worship, written by a priest from his deepest heart and soul whose one prayer is that this text has made a difference (great or small) in the life of the reader.

In the following prayers, I hope one can find that peace of the kingdom which the world cannot give. I sincerely pray that frequent meditations and reflections on this text will assist the reader to ponder – as did Our Lady – the great teaching events of the life of Jesus and His disciples and that this pondering action will result in the peace of Jesus Christ living in the soul of each reader. God bless you!

Amen!

PRAYERS

For a Happy Death

Jesus, I believe in You; I love You;
I want to serve You today, tomorrow – and always.
I'm aware of my sin.
I know my faults and my failings.
Help me to live and to work today for You.

Please take care of my loved ones, especially
those closest to me in blood and friendship.
Lord, help those poor whose names are known to You.

Have mercy on the dying. Give them courage
*   to die well.*
Let all of us remember that
there is great difference between dying
and dying in the Lord.

Lord, if it is Your will that I die without
*   human company or human comfort, help*
*   me to die in You.*
There is all the world's difference
between dying and dying in the Lord.

Let me celebrate my life by dying a holy death
in Your arms and in the company
of Your Mother and Saint Joseph.

Amen!

When Lonely

Lord Jesus Christ, living today is so much
like being alone in the middle of a crowd:
People don't really listen to one another;
people don't really hear what each is saying.
Help me, O Lord, to listen to my sisters and
brothers when, in their need, they seek me out.

Help me to be a true companion of the needy.
Lord, loneliness comes not from being alone
but from feeling "shut out" by people.
Never let me be too attached to some people
to the exclusion of others.
Lord, let me welcome You living in my
sisters and brothers. Let me hear their story.
Lord, let me always be kind, generous and
open to all.

Amen!

The Sacred Heart

Jesus, the flames leaping from Your Heart
And the pulsating beat of Your heart, represent
What Your Father gives to all of us who believe.
The cross surmounting Your heart and the crown
Of thorns piercing Your heart represent what
We have given to You, pain and sorrow.

Jesus, let me try to remove Your pain and
Sorrow by living a life of reparation for the
Sins of others. In so doing, I will truly

Practice genuine Christian love. Help me, Lord,
To adore You as You live in my sisters
And my brothers.

Jesus, living in Mary, come live in me.
Jesus, loving in Mary, come love in me.
Jesus, redeeming the world of today, help
Me to live as a redeemed Christian,
Within Your sacred heart.

Amen!

The Immaculate Heart

O Mary, Immaculate Mother of Jesus, my Savior,
you were the last gift of Your Son from
His cross of pain.
O Mary, you were present to Jesus throughout
His life, never leaving His side. Even
in death, you were with Him.
Dearest Mother, surely He was always with you.
Your immaculate heart helped Him to
understand our all too human hearts.
His sacred heart was formed within your
immaculate heart.
Dear Mother, teach me as you taught Him.
Loving Mother, love me as you loved Him.
Holy Mother, when at last I die, let your
Jesus say to me: "I've heard my Mother
speak lovingly of you."

Amen!

To Saint Joseph

Loving Saint Joseph, guardian of Jesus and Mary,
Your entire life with your wife and step-Son,
was a challenge.
Help me in the challenges of my life to live
as a faithfilled disciple of Jesus and son/daughter
of Mary.
Help me to make those choices that benefit
the coming of God's kingdom here on earth.
Let me stand up in defense of the sacredness
of life at all levels and stages: from the
moment of conception to the final event of death.
Let me, when my hour comes, die in the arms
of Jesus and Mary and in your loving presence,
dearest Saint Joseph, my guardian and friend.

Amen!